TRUTH BOOKS PRESENTS:
SATAN'S SINISTER SCHEME FOR HUMANITY'S DEMISE
Volume 1

Written By:

Jonathan Jones

Table Of Contents:

Introduction...2
        Now The Truth
        The Purpose
        The Lord Instruction to Me
        Dream & Interpretation
        How to use this book
        Reopening the case against demons
        Good news for born-again believers

I. Understanding Lucifer's character while in heaven............6

II. Demons are spirits but with human-like personalities.........29

III. Satan's false light 42

IV. Misconceptions about demons and possessions 49

V. Spiritual warfare 74

VI. Children of demons 92

VII. Seasonal Attacks 94

VIII. Demons and mental illnesses...................................105

IX. Know thou enemies 106

X. Doctrine of demons for the last days...........................115

XI. Satan's plans...121

XII. Christian's spiritual weapons and armors......................136

Introduction:

Are there aliens among us? This burning question has captured the imagination of countless individuals. The concept of extraterrestrial life has long fascinated humanity, prompting a quest to uncover the truth behind the existence of beings from other planets.

Aliens, in popular culture, are often depicted as intelligent, technologically advanced life forms hailing from distant galaxies or dimensions. While concrete evidence remains elusive, many firmly believe that aliens could exist in various forms, ranging from humanoid beings to entirely different, unimaginable shapes.

Speculation about aliens living among us provokes both excitement and skepticism. Some argue that alien civilizations have covertly infiltrated human society, disguising themselves as ordinary individuals to learn about our culture and study our behavior. These supposed aliens might possess mind-bending abilities or advanced technology, enabling them to blend seamlessly into our daily lives.

Some have proclaimed that aliens adducted them, and once captured, actually preformed some experimentations on their brain and body; and once finished, tormented them. But could these things be true? Could other intelligent life forms entered into our world and have performed such tasks upon certain people?

Now The Truth:

While we have no concrete evidence whether aliens are currently walking among us, we do have conformation that another entity does; and they are actively warring against all of humanity.

In the depths of darkness, lurking behind veils of malevolence, lies Satan's wicked plot for the downfall of humanity. With unfathomable malevolence, Satan, the embodiment of evil, has crafted an array of plans aimed at ensnaring and corrupting the souls of all humans. Unbeknownst to the unsuspecting masses, these nefarious machinations seek to plunge the world into eternal chaos and despair.

Understanding Satan's evil plans is no longer an option, but is of necessity for our modern era. Satan, the meticulous deceiver, crafts wicked strategies to ensnare the unsuspecting souls. His diabolical schemes aim to fragment our faith, instilling doubt and leading astray even the most virtuous hearts. Satan's ultimate goal is to corrupt the pure essence of our being, planting the seeds of temptation that flourish into evil actions.

To comprehend Satan's malevolent intentions, one must delve into the depths of his twisted psyche. He capitalizes on our weaknesses, exploiting the very vulnerabilities we may underestimate. His web of deceit spans across various realms, manipulating desires, distorting perceptions, and fostering chaos. Armed with eternal patience, he meticulously orchestrates his sinister plans, gradually eroding the moral fabric of humanity.

At times, Satan hides in plain sight, disguising his intentions behind attractive illusions and false promises. He tempts us with immediate gratification, blinding us to the long-term consequences of our choices. Recognizing his tactics requires vigilance and spiritual discernment, for his destructive agenda lurks within the shadows of our desires.

To counter Satan's wicked plans, we must arm ourselves by putting on the entire armor of Yahweh and walk in His Spirit daily. By submitting ourselves to Yeshua teachings, we gain the power to resist his allure. Unmasking Satan's darkness is not for the faint-hearted, but through unwavering faith, steadfast prayer, and seeking divine guidance, we can safeguard our souls from his treacherous grasp.

Purpose:

The main objective of this compelling book is to shed light on the hidden realm of devils, compelling readers to become offended with them and to take up arms against their malevolent kingdom and wicked works. Delving deep into the dark waters of supernatural forces, it reveals a startling truth: every pain endured, illness suffered, every crime committed, heartbreak, every lie told, and beloved lost can ultimately be attributed to these insidious entities. Demons, driven by a ruthless and unimaginable hatred, yearn for nothing more than to inflict suffering upon humanity, consigning them to the eternal fires of hell.

Through gripping narratives and insightful analysis, this book unveils the methods through which demons operate within our world, elucidating their tactics, strategies, and insidious influences. It emboldens readers to recognize the signs of their malevolence, empowering them to resist and fight back against their demonic assaults. By meticulously exposing the true nature of these tormentors, the book equips readers with the knowledge and understanding necessary to safeguard themselves and their loved ones from the clutches of these infernal beings. Prepare to embark on a transformative journey that will awaken your spirit and fortify you in the battle against the demonic forces that seek to enslave us all.

"Whoever makes a practice of sinning is of the devil, for the devil has been sinning from the beginning. The reason the Son of God appeared was to destroy the works of the devil," **1ˢᵗ John 3:8 ESV.**

The Greek word for "Destroy" is [Lúō 3089] which means: *to dissolve, destroy*. The dictionary word for "*dissolve*" is: *disperse* {to cause to break up, *disappear* {to pass from view or to cease to be}, *destroy* {to ruin the structure, organic existence, or condition of or to ruin as if by tearing to shreds}. Therefore, as a believer and servant of Yeshua, the sin nature has no business governing over our lives. Ergo, by what He has done for us, abiding in sin is a choice, not force!

Jesus paid too high a price upon the cross for us to simply allow sin to continue ruling over our lives. He willingly left his heavenly position and endured the immense shame and agony on our behalf. The ultimate sacrifice he made for our sins was by giving his very life. Jesus poured out his blood so that we could be set free from the chains of a sinful lifestyle. He bore the weight of our transgressions so that we could experience the fullness of redemption and a restored relationship with God. It is through his selfless act that we have the opportunity to walk in the light of his grace, free from the power of sin. May we never forget the tremendous price Jesus paid, and may we strive each day to live in the liberty and victory he secured for us.

One of the reasons Yeshua [Jesus] was manifest, that He might destroy the works of the devil and therefore, if you're a believer in Yeshua, then you must kill the works of Satan in your own life.

The Lord's Instructions To Me:

One day, I was told how some Christians were engaging in debauchery and the news was unsettling to me. Afterwards, I went into prayer and My Lord God spoke to my heart and said, *"Many of my people are doing things that they shouldn't be, and are fighting one another, instead of battling against demons."* And before I could ask Him why, He said to me,
"It is because they don't know enough about Satan, is to fight against him and his angels." Then He said, *"But I will reveal the Devil and his unholy angels to you, that you may despise them and then, reveal them unto my people."*

To be totally honest, I exposed the devil to certain individuals, but shortly afterward, I stopped, due to coming under heavy attacks by them and at that time, I didn't have people standing in prayer and fasting for me.

Dream Of Mine: Prior to having this particular dream, I had veer off from certain things of Yahweh.
Comment: I will not reveal the totality of this dream, meaning that there were additional scenes, but I will not reveal them at this time, but only the part I consider relevant to this subject.
In the dream, I removed myself from the saints and followed after a thing that was pleasing to my own eyes.
Then I entered on the back of a pickup truck, along with others, and we were taking to what looked like a desert place. Then, the driver began backing up the pickup truck, until he reached a giant furnace; and started to raise the bay, and when he did this, everyone in the bay was bound hand and feet, and people begin rolling into the fiery furnace.

As I was about to enter into the big furnace, I called upon My Lord and God and immediately, a mighty hand and arm descended from heaven and grabbed my body, and I ascended into the first heaven.
Then I heard an audible voice say, *"I will send you back to earth and allow you to hear the devil's plans, then shall you reveal them unto my people."*
And when the voice said this to me, I was let back down to earth, and awaken from the dream.

Interpretation of this Dream:

The lust of the eyes, caused me to become impatient and move prematurely, and I went to please myself instead of my Lord God, and therefore, entered into something that I shouldn't have.
The desert place is where demons enjoy working; for it was in the desert where Satan fought against Yeshua [Jesus], **Matthew 4:1**. I gave into my temptation, instead of overcoming it by the precious blood of Yeshua.

The desert: At that point in my life, I felt like I was in a dry place and wasn't advancing.
When the truck was backing up, this represented that I was backsliding from Yahweh and returning to things that He had delivered me from.

When I and others were bound up, both hands and feet, this represented that if I didn't truly repent, I was going to be casted into the Lake of Fire; for the bible said that the lost souls, on the day of judgment, will be bound hands and feet [**Matthew 22:13**] and thrown into hell of fire.

I was saved because I cried out to My Lord and God [**Romans 10:13**]; this was the hand and arm that reached down and grabbed me.

The audible voice speaking to me was Yeshua, giving me my assignment. When I was let down from heaven, it meant that I must return back to the Lord's works.

My Prayer For You:

I pray that by the time you finish this book, you will take up spiritual arms against the works of the devil and that you will abhor demons with all of your heart, mind, body, and soul. And whenever you witness their vile works and propaganda, you will immediately enter into attack mode, and do battle against them. I pray that you will use this book to help educate those around you, and to promote this book, so like you, they too will become offended with devils and join you in your endeavor to battle them. And finally, I pray that Yeshua will reveal to you the hidden revelations that are in his book, to the ones He has chosen to unveil it to. Amen.

How To Use This Book:

This book is designed for educational purposes and as a work book. Each chapter is designed to greatly increase your knowledge and understanding about demons. You will be asked to participate in the lessons or exercises within this book. By participating in the lessons, they will enable you to visualize the fight needed to do spiritual warfare with the demons you will be encountering throughout your life, and to help you to better recall what to do when faced with a demonic situation. Therefore, it is highly recommended that you study the information and complete the lessons afterwards.

Additional Information: While most of the information presented in this book about demons comes directly from the bible, other bits of intel will come from my own personal experiences, other people's knowledge, and through revelation knowledge that God has graciously imparted to me. In addition, when

I want you to ponder something in particular, I will emphasize it by writing: "Something to think about." I believe it will encourage deeper contemplation and help you grasp profound insights. I have also included sections labeled "Mystery Revelation." This signifies that the Holy Spirit has divinely disclosed a mystery to me, and my intention is to share it with you. These moments of revelation are remarkable and should be approached with reverence, as they offer valuable understanding beyond what is explicitly stated in scriptures.

My aim is to provide a well-rounded perspective on the subject of demons, blending scriptural truths, personal encounters, wisdom shared by others, and hallowed truths revealed through the Holy Spirit. May this book illuminate your path and ignite your spiritual journey.

Good News For Born-Again Believers In Yeshua

As a born-again believer in Yeshua, you can rest assured that fear has no place in your life when it comes to the works of demons. Through the precious sacrifice of Jesus, who willingly gave His life for us, we have been granted an incredible power over all the forces of darkness.
With this divine authority, we possess the ability to bind the hands of the wicked ones, rendering them powerless in their schemes. No longer are we subject to their tactics or manipulation. Through Yeshua, we have been granted the power to break the chains that bind others, setting captives free from the clutches of darkness.

The assurance of this power is rooted in the eternal victory secured by Jesus' sacrifice. By accepting His love and salvation, we partake in the authority He bestowed upon us. It is a divine gift of grace, enabling us to overcome and walk confidently in the face of any demonic presence.

So, children of Yahweh, rejoice in the truth that you have nothing to fear. In Yeshua, we stand victorious, equipped to combat the works of evil and bring freedom to those held captive. Embrace this power, and step boldly into the incredible calling we have received.

Reopening The Case Against Demons

Special Favor: Before I begin making my case against devils/demons, would you join me in a little roleplay? I would like for you to view me as an ambassador for Yeshua and yourselves as world leaders; like the ones in the United Nations [UN]; because you are a leader in your home. And at this general assembly, the entire world is watching us, and based on your decision after I present to you these unwavering statements, firsthand evidence, and valid eyewitnesses, you, the general assembly must then decide whether to consider Satan and his minions an imminent threat and we go to war at once, or to whitewash him and his angels, and continue to allow them to finish their pernicious works. With that being said, let us proceed!

Ladies and gentlemen of the general assembly, today I stand before you as the ambassador of the kingdom of Yahweh in the case against all devils. I urge you to view me as your advocate, presenting evidence that will reveal the true nature of these malevolent beings. In this assembly, God himself presides as the ultimate Judge, watching over our proceedings.

The purpose of my opening statement is simple yet profound: to provide undeniable proof that you should abhor and repudiate these devils with every fiber of your being. Throughout this trial, I will shed light on their treachery, exposing their betrayal while they resided in the heavenly realm.

But their evil intentions didn't stop there. No, they had far more sinister plans for all of humanity. Their wicked schemes have caused untold suffering and despair throughout history. It is our duty, as enlightened individuals, to rise against these malevolent forces and fight them relentlessly until the end of our days.
Join me, esteemed members of the assembly, as we embark on this arduous journey of unveiling the truth.

Let empathy, righteousness, and the pursuit of justice guide our proceedings, and may the weight of their wrongdoing be brought to light.

Together, we will strive to ensure that their vile existence is forever repudiated and condemned. And after I am finish, may we all attack them from every side and direction.

CASE ONE: Understanding Satan's Character

In order for us to comprehensively grasp Lucifer and his fallen angels' current and future plans, it becomes essential to examine their original intentions while they were still in heaven. Lucifer, driven by a desire to be equal to Yahweh, his creator, deviated from seeking after God's heart and instead envied His hand of power. This envy propelled Lucifer to lead other angels astray, for anyone who did not feel as he did would not have joined him in his rebellion. Lucifer's initial aspiration to achieve equal status with God highlights the depth of his discontent with his existing position in heaven.

By delving into Lucifer's mindset during his time in heaven, we can gain crucial insights into his motivations and objectives as the fallen angel. Understanding the root causes behind his rebellion allows us to better analyze his strategies and plans unfolding in the present and future.

In this chapter, you will learn these things:

- The meaning of Lucifer/Hêlēl's name
- What caused Lucifer/Hêlēl to fall in the first place.
- what was his original plan while in heaven
- What Lucifer said that caused one-third of the heavenly angels to turn from Yahweh
- The judgment that Yahweh pronounced upon them
- Lucifer's character seen through animals, amphibians, and insect

By understanding these things, I believe we can understand his diabolical plots for what's to come about within these last days.
Then secondly, we need to view his personality by looking at some of the animals, amphibians, and insects that Satan and his demons are compared to in the Bible.

Lucifer/Hêlēl
- Lucifer's name means: "morning star" and "light-bearer" and "day star"
Origin: Latin
- Hêlēl's name means the same.
Origin: Hebrew

First of all, Lucifer/ Hêlēl's sin didn't occur when he caused Adam and Eve to sin, but rather when he and his unholy demons where in heaven, when they were good and loving angels.

What Cause Lucifer/Hêlēl to Fall?

Lucifer's Physical Beauty: *"Your heart was lifted [**Pride**] up because of your beauty…"* **Ezekiel 28:17**. While most ministers believe Lucifer's first sin was pride, but as you have just read, it was his own beauty that caused arrogance to elevate him. Ergo, the beginning of his fall was him admiring his own beauty [*self-glory*], and then, pride. Lucifer was absolutely perfect in beauty. Think of his great beauty as gasoline and his pride as fire, and we all know how well gas and fire mix together.

Modern Times: Satan works primarily through beauty. Think about the beauty pageant, and while they would have their viewers to believe that the contest is being judged on a number of things like: personality, intelligence, talent, and answering judge's questions, we know that the competition is primarily based on the women's outer beauty and what she is wearing. Satan desires to show the external beauty in things in order to entrap people, to enslave him or her, that they will be his personal slaves until they die and then, burn in hell.

"You have corrupted your wisdom by reason of your brightness…" **Ezekiel 28:17**. The next thing to help corrupt Lucifer was his brightness, which caused his great wisdom to become defile.

Modern Times: Let's keep things real, the fairer a person's skin color is, the more opportunities they will have within this corrupt worldly system. And as long as Satan and his demons are at play, racism will continue to exist. Demons have been very successful in dividing the human race, all due to the color of someone's skin tone, hair texture, and vocabulary.

Satan and his demons, the embodiment of evil, play a significant role in fueling the racism that persists in the world today. Racism, in its profound darkness, has caused immeasurable division, forced labor, separation, and unfathomable brutality leading to the untimely deaths of millions throughout history.

It is Satan, the prince of discord, who whispers notions of superiority and inferiority into the hearts of humanity, igniting the flames of racial hatred. His demons, haunting society's collective consciousness, manipulate individuals and perpetuate discriminatory ideologies. They take pleasure in nurturing prejudice, sowing seeds of animosity, encouraging systemic racism, and fostering divisions among people.

Racism's poisonous tendrils have entwined themselves into various facets of society, tearing apart the very fabric of human unity. The horrors of forced labor and modern-day slavery, the tragic consequences of racial segregation, and the countless lives cruelly claimed by racially-motivated violence all bear witness to its destructive power.

Racism has sadly infiltrated the walls of numerous churches, where an alarming number of white individuals refuse to accept a minister of color. Equally distressing is the fact that there are some black congregants who hesitate to sit under the guidance of a white minister. These divisive attitudes rooted in racism undoubtedly inflict deep wounds on the unity and teachings of Jesus Christ.

It is crucial to remember that our salvation lies not in the color of Jesus's skin, but in the redemptive power of his precious blood. As followers of Christ, we are called to embrace love, compassion, and acceptance, disregarding the superficial boundaries that divide us. Racism within the church tarnishes the very essence of Jesus's message and hinders our ability to truly live out his teachings.

Let us strive to create churches that genuinely reflect the love and inclusivity of Jesus Christ. May we reject racism in all its forms and work towards healing the wounds inflicted by discrimination, standing together as one body in Christ.

To confront racism means understanding its origin beyond mere human agency, acknowledging the spiritual forces working behind the scenes. Only by recognizing Satan's sinister influence can we stand united against racial injustice, battling with love, compassion, and unwavering commitment to create a world free from the clutches of bigotry and hatred.

The vast majority of people who believe in the existence of angels, automatically assumes that they're white angelic beings, but nowhere in scripture does the bible say that all of them are. In fact, the only thing that it says about their skin complexion is, that they shine with the glory of Yahweh on them [**Luke 2:9**]. Other than that, they can look like humans [**Acts 1:10**]. But there are angels that look totally different than humans, having faces of different kinds of animals.

Therefore, angels, when coming in the form of humans, can be any kind of color and race. In the bible, they never came in the form of women, only men, but if Yahweh so desire for them to come in such a form, they can, because they're not humans.
The bible informs us to be careful how we entertain strangers, because some have unwittingly entertained angels, thinking that they were humans. [**Hebrews 13:2**].

Dreams and Open Visions of Mine: *I have seen angels, both in dreams and while awake, some had fair skin, while other ones had darker skin, or the color of black men. The ones I seen, could have been the same angel, just taking on different skin complexions.*

True Story: On one Wednesday night bible study, I and my mother attended church. I noticed my mother rubbing her hand, but thought nothing of it until we left service that night, and she told me this story.

She said that before entering the church, her right hand was hurting very much. The pain was getting to the point where she thought about going to the doctor, but decided to come to church first.

Upon entering the church, she was greeted by two usherettes and then my mother went and sat down. Then the head of the usherettes, came and asked my mother is she okay. My mother informed her of the great pain that was in her right hand. Then the usherette took my mother by the hand that was hurting and started praying over it. After the prayer, she began talking with my mom; but during their conversation, the usherette continued to massage her hand, the entire time.

After a few minutes, she smiled at mom and then left. My mother noticed that her hand didn't hurt anymore. So, she immediately arose and went to the usherette, to thank her for praying and massaging her hand until the pain was gone, and to let her know that God had healed her.

While thanking her for praying and massaging her hand until the great pain had left, the whole time, the usherette was looking at my mom, as if she was surprised and didn't know what she was talking about.

Then she said to my mother, "sister Jones, I don't know what you're talking about. I greeted you at the door when you came in, but the whole time, I have been sitting back here at the door, talking with another usherette. *I haven't moved from my seat. And the other usherette confirmed her story.*

My mother then realized that Yahweh had sent one of His angels, in the form of the usherette, is to heal her hand.
I was there that night, but because I was sitting in a different location, I didn't see any of this. Now, while there's no mention of angels being women in the bible, this doesn't mean that they cannot transform into one.

"*You were perfect in your ways from the day that you were created, till iniquity was found in you,*" **Ezekiel 28:15**.

The final thing that corrupted Lucifer/Hêlēl was ***iniquity***, embedded in his heart. But let's understand what this iniquity is. Iniquities [Heb. 5766] Perverseness, wickedness, dishonesty, wrong, injustice, unrighteous, depravity; to distort (morally); to deal unjustly. So, now we know exactly what's inside of Satan/Lucifer's wicked heart. The nine things I just named, replaced the nine stones that Yahweh gave to him before his fall. Lucifer wore nine stones on his breastplate [**Ezekiel 28:13**].

Revelation Knowledge: So, if you had insight in the spirit, you would see Satan's new breastplate, which consist of these nine wicked black stones:

First Row:
Pride Black Stone
Perverseness Black Stone
Wicked Black Stone

Second Row:
Dishonesty Black Stone
Wrong Black Stone
Injustice Black Stone

Third Row:
Unrighteous Black Stone
Depravity Black Stone
Distort Morally Black Stone

These nine black stones distorted his perfection, causing his identity to change from the glory that was bestowed upon him, to the essence of darkness itself. The nine black stone makeup the characteristic of Lucifer; they unveil the truth about what's in his heart.

Caution: I heard a self-proclaimed prophet say out of ignorance, that Satan cannot create anything. This kind of thinking and speaking is both reckless and dangerous. I don't know about his god, but my Lord and Savior didn't create hatred, racism, perverseness, lies, and such like. Are who created witchcraft, did not Satan create the words for them to say and give the designs for what objects that would be needed for their services?

All that my God created was good according to Genesis chapter 1. Anyway, lets understand the meaning of these wicked stones, and how Satan used them on the fallen angels, and how he's using them in these last days.

Pride Black Stone: The First Stone of Lucifer, known as the "Pride Black Stone," represents the pinnacle of Lucifer's self-importance. Lucifer's pride swelled within him, leading him to greatly exaggerate his self-esteem. His arrogance drove him to believe that he and God should be equals, each ruling over their respective halves of heaven.

Fueled by this delusion, Lucifer's pride pushed him to challenge the very foundations of divinity. He refused to accept his place as a subordinate being and craved a power that equaled God's. This desire for supremacy birthed the idea of a celestial equality that would see him wield unfathomable authority and dominion.

The Pride Black Stone embodies the audacity of Lucifer's ambition, symbolizing his yearning for absolute sovereignty. It serves as a cautionary reminder of the dangers of hubris and the consequences that arise when one's pride blinds them to the eternal order.

Pride Stone Used Against Angels: How Lucifer used his "Pride Black Stone" on the fallen angels? Through the Pride Stone, Lucifer caused one-third of the angels to believe that they, like himself, were smarter, better looking, and deserved merit as himself. He convinced them of their self-importance and did praise the works of their hands. He redirected the glory that belonged to Yahweh, toward their own capabilities, promoting the ideal that they should believe in themselves, instead of in Yahweh, who created and gave them their abilities.

Pride Black Stone Used Against Humans: Generations Millennials [1981-1996], generation z [1997-2012] to generation alpha [2013-2028]; the vast majority of these generational workers, have a sense of entitlement;

believing and acting like those around them owed them something, when they haven't done anything to earn it. Most, but not all of them, work ethics is below average, and what little work they do, behave as if they've done much and complain about their pay, as if they should be compensated more. The pride stone as even caused many of them to think they should be promoted to a leadership position; other people should be working for them, instead of them working.

The bible says, *"Pride goes before destruction, and a haughty spirit before a fall,"* **Proverbs 16:18**. Pride will always lead to destruction and causes one to fall. But the main thing pride causes, is a person to exalt themselves above the knowledge of Yahweh.

Perverseness Black Stone: The Second black stone that Lucifer wears is famously known as "The Perverseness Black Stone." It symbolizes his inclination to turn away from what is right or good, signifying his defiance towards Yahweh. This stone represents a manifestation of improper actions, incorrect choices, stubbornness, and obstinacy. Lucifer, the fallen angel, takes immense pride in possessing this stone, as it epitomizes his rebellion against divine authority. It serves as a constant reminder of his self-proclaimed freedom and independence, even though it leads him further away from the path of righteousness. This black stone, charged with the essence of perverseness, serves as a potent emblem of Lucifer's deviation from the divine plan and his unwavering resolve to chart his own destiny.

Perverseness Black Stone Used Against Angels: Lucifer persuade the fallen angels that under his rule and kingdom, they could choose for themselves what's right and good; that they didn't need God for such a thing. He told them that through him, and him alone, could he open their eyes and liberate them, as he had been freed. Those who bought into his lies, believed that his new profound knowledge, could actually empower and free them.

Perverseness Black Stone Used Against Humans: Satan used the voice of the serpent to informed Eve that, if they ate from the tree of the knowledge of good and evil, their eyes would be opened; he caused them to believe that it was only through listening to him, could they obtain true knowledge, and then could they actually be like God.

In today's world, this lie is still prevalent, "you can choose for yourself what is good or not, and trust your heart," when the bible informs us not to trust the heart [**Jeremiah 17:9**], because it is deceitful. Ever since humans have decided for themselves what is good versus evil, especially in my country, many cannot even define what's a woman now, and some are so delusional, that they believe that transgender man, who's pretending to be a woman, can actually become pregnant; how ironic is that!

Wickedness Black Stone: The Third Black Stone that Lucifer wears is known as "The Wickedness Black Stone." This stone holds the power to reveal the wickedness that proceeded from his heart. With its fierce and vicious nature, it symbolizes his capacity for mischief and roguish behavior. It serves as a reminder of his malevolent intentions and deceptive nature. This stone also unveils his ability to cause harm, distress, and trouble wherever he treads. Its dark energy reflects the depths of his malevolence and serves as a cautionary reminder of the dangers he presents. The "Wickedness Black Stone" encapsulates the essence of Lucifer's sinister presence, an ever-present reminder of the evil that lurks within his heart.

Wickedness Black Stone Used Against Angels: Through the knowledge of this stone, Lucifer prepared those who accepted his lies, how to do harm against the other angels, if war broke out between them. Lucifer was convinced that he would rule like Yahweh, even if it meant by force. So, then secretly, they trained and prepared themselves for battle and those who joined them not, after the battle, would be forced to serve Lucifer and his armies for all eternity.

Wickedness Black Stone Used Against Humans: Through this stone, Satan has put into the hearts of some to be an abuser: physically, mentally, sexually, and verbally, to kill the innocent [those who have no voices], to become a terrorist, murderer, and others to commit genocide.

Dishonesty Black Stone: The Fourth Black Stone that Lucifer wears is known as "The Dishonesty Black Stone." This stone symbolizes the absence of honesty or integrity, reflecting his disposition to defraud or deceive. As the embodiment of deceit, Lucifer employs this stone's power to carry out his fraudulent schemes. It amplifies his cunning nature, allowing him to manipulate and trick others effortlessly. With the Dishonesty Black Stone at his disposal, he orchestrates elaborate scams that exploit even the smallest vulnerabilities in his victims. This stone's dark energy feeds into Lucifer's insatiable desire to exploit the trust of others and revels in the chaos and destruction that follows. Those who encounter the Dishonesty Black Stone should remain vigilant, for its malevolent influence can lead even the most pure-hearted astray.

Dishonesty Black Stone Used Against Angels: Through this stone, Lucifer was able to teach his followers how to lie and be dishonest toward other angels, something that, until that time, they were totally unaware of. He showed them how to scam other angels out of the things that Yahweh had blessed them with.
He even convinced them that by obeying him, no harm from Yahweh will they face. Satan just didn't start being a thief and liar when he arrived on earth, no, this started while he was still in heaven.

Revelation Knowledge: Just as Satan's son, Judas Iscariot was pilfering funds from Yeshua [**John 12:6**], Lucifer was stealing treasures from Yahweh while in heaven. The old saying is true, "Like father, like son!" And this is why Yeshua calls Satan both a thief and liar.

Dishonesty Black Stone Used Against Humans: Just like the serpent was dishonest with Eve, Satan has used this stone to help create many false religions around the world; causing the people to believe that there are many different ways to God [Yahweh], when Yeshua clearly said, *"I am the way, the truth, and the life, no man [person] comes unto the Father, except through me,"* [**John 14:6**].

<u>TRUTH THAT HURTS!</u> Yeshua said, *"for except you believe that I am he, you shall die in your sins,"* **John 8:24**. This means that EVERY RELIGION that doesn't believe that Yeshua is the Christ, and accepts Him, whenever they die and face judgment, they're going directly to the Lake of Fire or Hell.

Wrongness Black Stone: The Fifth Black Stone that Lucifer wears, often referred to as "The Wrongness Black Stone," serves as a symbol that represents the injurious, unfair, or unjust actions and conduct of the fallen angel. It is a manifestation of Lucifer's desire to inflict harm upon others without any legitimate provocation or just cause. This dark stone reveals his willingness to violate and invade the legal rights of others, showcasing his profound disregard for justice and fairness.

As Lucifer adorns himself with this stone, it serves as a constant reminder of his malevolent intentions and his inclination towards perpetrating acts that cause suffering and imbalance. Its presence signifies the malevolence that lurks within him, a blatant defiance of the principles of righteousness and equity. The Wrongness Black Stone stands as a chilling testament to the nefarious deeds that Lucifer seeks to carry out, embodying the very essence of his misguided and destructive aspirations.

Wrongness Black Stone Used Against Angels: Lucifer used this stone is to falsely accuse Yahweh to the angels, in hopes that they would view Him wrong. *"Behold, He [Yahweh] puts no trust in His servants; and His angels He charged with folly,"* **Job 4:18**. Lucifer poisoned those angels who followed him with the ideal that Yahweh didn't trust and believed in them, but he would trust them if they pledge their allegiances to him and share his kingdom with them. He promised to allow them to have higher positions within his kingdom.

Wrongness Black Stone Used Against Humans: In today's world, daily, Satan is trying to convince the saints that Yahweh is ignoring their prayers and that's why they haven't received what they have been asking for; so why waste time praying to Him! Furthermore, Satan is trying to persuade people that Yahweh doesn't trust them, no matter how faithful they are to Him. Furthermore, to those who he deems as worthy, to offer them the kingdoms of this world in exchange for their mind, spirit, and worship.

Injustice Black Stone: The Sixth Black Stone that Lucifer wears, known as "The Injustice Black Stone," symbolizes his relentless inclination to trample upon the rights of others. This dark stone acts as a reflection of his unwavering determination to impose his own will on the world. In Lucifer's realm, compromise or fair dealings hold no place. His perspective allows only for his own brand of justice, rendering any alternative as a blatant infringement upon the very essence of his existence. To him, any suggestion that deviates from his path is an assault on everything he stands for, and thus absolutely unacceptable and intolerable. The Injustice Black Stone stands as a testament to Lucifer's unwavering commitment to his principles, demonstrating how his actions challenge the very concept of justice itself.

Injustice Black Stone Used Against Angels: Lucifer proclaimed to those angels that Yahweh's ways, were actually infringing upon their rights, and if God was fair, then He wouldn't have a problem sharing the heavens with them; allowing Lucifer to rule and become His equal.

Mystery Revealed: If Lucifer would have achieved his goal, being equal with Yahweh, his next plan was to steal all the power and authority of Yahweh and to have the Creator to idolize him, but how can I prove this? Listen to what Satan [Lucifer] said to Yeshua, after showing Jesus the kingdoms of the world, and their glory, he said to him, *"All these I will give you, if you will fall down and worship me,"* **Matthew 4:9 ESV**.

The devil knew that Jesus was the Christ, the Son of God Himself: *"And devils also came out of many, crying out, and saying, you are Christ the Son of God. And He rebuking them, suffered them not to speak: for they knew that he was Christ,"* **Luke 4:41**. That's right, they knew that Jesus was God in flesh and yet, Satan requested that worshiped from Him.

Something to think about: Have you ever considered how truly terrible life would be if Lucifer had managed to achieve his wicked goal of being equal with God? The consequences would have been catastrophic. Lucifer, eventually, would have attempted to steal Yahweh's power, and making God to idolize him [Lucifer]. Just imagine the implications of that.

In today's world, things might seem bad at times, but we must not forget the unimaginable darkness that would have enveloped our existence if Satan and his demons had successfully replaced God. The very foundations of morality, integrity, and divine guidance would be shattered. The world as we know it would be unrecognizable.

Life, as we experience it now, is far from perfect, yet we still find solace in the love, compassion, and hope that God provides. The idea that such a source of benevolence could be replaced by malevolence is truly chilling. So, let us appreciate the presence of God, embrace His divine guidance, and ponder the immense blessings that come with His existence.

Injustice Black Stone Used Against Humans: In today's world, I have heard many say, *"If God is full of love and knows everything, then why does He allow so many to die in a hurricane or other natural disasters?"* Satan have blinded their eyes so that they aren't able to see that Yahweh has a plan for our lives, and how He thinks and does things, are oftentimes different than how we would do them. Next, we were bought with a price, and belong to Him [**1ˢᵗ Corinthians 6:19-20**]. The last time I checked, if I purchased something with my own money, I could do whatsoever I desired with it; this is also true with God.

Unrighteousness Black Stone: The Seventh Black Stone adorning Lucifer's formidable attire is referred to as "The Unrighteousness Black Stone." This sinister gem epitomizes the sinful, wicked, and unmerited acts committed by the notorious fallen angel. Holding the weight of unrepentant sins, the stone serves as a chilling reminder of the unyielding allure of temptation and the destructive power hidden within. As Lucifer parades this unholy charm, the whispers of its malevolent essence resonate throughout the realms, a chilling testament to the depths of his diabolical nature.

Unrighteousness Black Stone Used Against Angels: Lucifer taught his angels how to do the things that are not right in the sight of the Lord God. As before, but he took them deeper into those things that were wicked before Yahweh. He taught them how to trust and rely upon their heart, for what they considered to be righteousness, instead of trusting in what Yahweh had told them already.

Unrighteousness Black Stone Used Against Humans: In today's world, Satan is speaking through the mouths of motivative speakers, telling their listeners to trust their heart and the universe, which is nothing more than a doctrine of demons. A person's heart is deceitfully [**Jeremiah 17:9**] and the universe can no more bless a person, than the sands on beaches.

Comment: This is one of the main reasons why divorcements are so high around the world, because instead of the other person willing to listen and put themselves in their partner's shoes, they're too busy trying to prove how right they are; and will link themselves with either a family member or friend, who's willing to help validate their rightness. In **Judges 21:25** the bible says, "In those days there was no king in Israel. Everyone did what was right in his own eyes. I like to say, when the Holy Spirit is not dwelling in a person, but only religious ideals or they're a disbeliever, they will do whatsoever is right in their own eyes.

Depravity Black Stone: The Eighth Black Stone that Lucifer wears is known as 'The Depravity Black Stone.' This enigmatic stone holds an extraordinary power, hiding Lucifer's moral corruptive acts and practices. As Lucifer adorned this stone, it became a symbol of his malevolent influence.
With its malefic aura, 'The Depravity Black Stone' conceals the sinister truths hidden beneath Lucifer's deceptive facade. It acts as a tinted window into his twisted machinations, disguising his manipulation, temptation, and the defilement of righteousness. The stone's impenetrable blackness reverberates the echoes of countless souls corrupted by Lucifer's seductive whispers and destructive allure.

Depravity Black Stone Used Against Angels: Through this stone, Lucifer was able to teach his angels how to engage in corruptive behavior while in heaven, and then after, to conceal that corruption.

Depravity Black Stone Used Against Humans: This stone was used in the days of Noah [**Genesis 6:11**], so is it happening in today's world. Whenever you see mass corruption in a certain area, region, country, it's because that nations of people have bowed down and kiss the ring of Satan, and he, in returned, has reflected this black stone upon them; causing them to make much gains through deceptions.

Distort Morally Black Stone: The Nineth Black Stone that Lucifer wears is known as "The Distort Morally Black Stone." This malevolent stone possesses a twisted power, causing its bearer to delve into the realms of moral ambiguity. Its influence compels individuals to rationalize their actions, to convince themselves that their deeds, however ethically questionable, are warranted. Justifications are offered, providing a seemingly valid explanation for their past choices. It is a stone that manipulates perception, leading its subjects down a treacherous path paved with deception and faulty reasoning.

Those who fall under its sway are prone to taking a failing course of action, the consequences of which can be dire. The Distort Morally Black Stone weaves a web of moral confusion, distorting the boundaries between right and wrong. It whispers insidious whispers, nudging its wearer towards acts that, in truth, only hasten their demise.

Distort Morally Black Stone Used Against Angels: Through this stone, Lucifer taught his angels how to distort the truth, in a way that seemed very believable, in order to gain the advantage over other angels. They became unresponsible and questioned the motive of other angels.

Distort Morally Black Stone Used Against Humans: Lucifer uses this stone to eliminate morals and values in today's world; and as a result, it has empowered the mindset of, "*do whatsoever feels right, and in doing so, you have freed yourself*!" In addition, it has caused many to rationalize and redirect the blame on someone else, rather than accepting responsibilities for their actions.

Something to think about: this stone is perhaps used the most. Just look at how easy it is for a person to lie, and not just to a stranger, but to the very person they claim to love and care about. They can lie as easy as they are able to breathe; effortless!

*"You have **defiled** your **sanctuaries** by the multitude of **your iniquities**, by the iniquity of your traffic…"* **Ezekiel 28:18**. Iniquity [Heb. 5771] Âwōn: this same word is linked to the iniquities previously revealed. In the past, Lucifer had a certain place where he would go and worship the Lord God, but when iniquities from his own heart emerged, it defiled that location.

Satan's Secret Agents With the Church

Lucifer was an anointed Cherub [**Ezekiel 28:14**], but what kind of an anointing does he has on his life as of now? He has an evil anointing. But lets us understand the occurrent anointing that is upon him and his demons. Remember that Satan is a copycat of God, trying to mimic the Lord's system, but in an evil way. So, lets us read **Isaiah 61:1-3**.

"The Spirit of the Lord God is upon me; because the Lord has anointed me to preach good tidings unto the meek; he has sent me to bind up the brokenhearted, to proclaim liberty to the captives, and the opening of the prison to them that are bound; to proclaim the acceptable year of the Lord, and the day of vengeance of our God; to comfort all that mourn; to appoint unto them that mourn in Zion, to give unto them beauty for ashes, the oil of joy for mourning, the garment of praise for the spirit of heaviness; that they might be called trees of righteousness, the planting of the Lord, that he might be glorified."

<u>*Now, let's rewrite this, to sound demonic:*</u>

The spirit of uncleanness is upon his servants; because Satan has anointed them to preach lies and compromising messages unto who have a form of godliness and disobedience. He has sent them to victimize the brokenhearted, to proclaim false freedom to those already in captivity, and to keep the prison doors closed, those who are enslaved already. To proclaim the year that sin should be accepted. And the day of Satan's wrath upon all of those who oppose him. To bring additional discomfort to those who are already grieving. To give them sadness in exchange for their happiness, the wine of drunkenness in exchange for the person's soberness, the spirit of heaviness in exchange for peace of mind, that they might be called the children of the wicked one, for the uses of his services.

Lucifer, the fallen angel, has defiled his sanctuary and now seeks to corrupt our modern churches. He employs a cohort of individuals, whom I refer to as Satan's Secret Agents (SSAs), to infiltrate and weaken the church from within. These agents are highly skilled and trained soldiers for the devil, equipped with the very assets that attract the average church: wealth, talent, attractiveness, and helpfulness.

At first glance, they appear innocent, but their true motive is nothing short of deadly and destructive. Their modus operandi involves befriending as many church members as possible, gaining their trust and extracting valuable information about the pastor. Armed with this knowledge, they worm their way into the pastor's inner circle, capturing his trust, ears, and ultimately, his heart.

Once they gain power within the church, these agents start subtly implementing Satan's desires. These agents weren't sent with the intent to have that church close its doors, no, but rather to have certain messages omitted from their teaching and or preaching. Subjects like: the blood of the lamb, testimonies about overcoming demons, strength in crucifying the flesh, what grace is really about, deliverance, and exposing the tricks of the devil are strictly prohibited. But rather, the teacher or preacher must talk about things that make their members feel good about themselves, in spite of how their living. They must teach: "as long as you're doing your best, God understands, and you are okay." And "It's okay to hang out with sinners, even Jesus did so." Instead of telling them that Jesus ministered to them about God, rebuked their sins, and then departed.

If the pastor resists their manipulations, they withdraw, taking with them their vast financial contributions. This departure causes a domino effect, with disillusioned members following suit and leaving the church. Beware, for these SSAs are masterful deceivers, aiming to compromise biblical doctrine and weaken the church. Stay vigilant, and guard against the subtle infiltration of evil that aims to defile our sacred places.

Satan's Secret Agents are Trained In: • Euphemism • Causing Duplicity • Dissimulation
• Dupery • Rebellion Against Spiritual Authority • Sowing Discord within the body of Christ
• Skilled in the Art of Deception • Forming Occults & Forms of godliness • Eliciting a person pass mistake • False Flag Operation

The devil has also employed some pastors to become his SSAs, and they're assigned to attack other ministers of God. Instead of them helping to restore a fallen brother or sister in the Lord, they behave and treat them like the world does, with disdain.

*"By the multitude of your **merchandise** they **have filled** the midst of **you with violence**, and **you have sinned**…"* **Ezekiel 28:16**. While in heaven, before the fall of humans, and when iniquities entered into Lucifer's heart, he begins conducting business in his sanctuary, the place where he should have been worshipping and praising Yahweh.

This kind of behavior was also going on in Jesus' era. In **Matthew 21:12-13**, *"And Jesus entered the temple of Yahweh, and cast out all them that sold and bought in the temple, and overthrew the tables of the money-changers, and the seats of them that sold doves. And said unto them, "It is written, my house shall be called the house of prayer; but you have made it a den of thieves."*

In **John 2:15**, Jesus made a scourge of small cords, and drove out those who sold sheep and oxen. This was the only time that Jesus became so angry and displeased with their behavior, that He put actions with His anger, droving them out of His Father's house. The religious people within the temple, where more focused on selling and making money, then helping the people to connect with Yahweh and have a closer walk with Him. Whenever you see this kind of behavior occurring within the church, its due to several SSAs that have been planted within.

Now you know the things that caused Lucifer to fall from the grace of Yahweh. But, from the beginning of this book, I said that I will play the part of an ambassador and you, the world's leaders. With that being said, I will need to write this as a story, giving you [the assembly] as greater point of view.

Story of Lucifer's Downfall:

<u>Revelation Knowledge</u>: Lucifer, seeing his own reflection in still water, became overwhelmed by his own unparalleled beauty and brightness, began to glorify himself above all else. With unmatched elegance and charm, he believed himself to be the epitome of beauty, surpassing even the angels. His flawless features and radiant aura made him incomparable.

His heart swelled with an overwhelming sense of pride as he believed himself to be the pinnacle of aesthetic perfection, surpassing the allure of every other celestial being. No angel could challenge his undeniable charm and magnetic allure.

Not only did Lucifer consider himself incomparably beautiful, but he also viewed himself as the epitome of wisdom. He boasted of his unrivaled intellect, convinced that his understanding surpassed that of any other angelic being. His mind, sharper than a thousand swords, seemed to grasp the intricacies of the universe effortlessly, granting him an unassailable superiority. No question was too perplexing for him to answer, no conundrum too complex for his profound intellect. He saw himself as the embodiment of wisdom, surpassing the knowledge of every other celestial being.

But it wasn't just his physical allure that filled Lucifer with pride. As pride consumed him further, Lucifer deemed himself the superior leader among the celestial host. He stood proudly, bearing the title of the anointed Cherub, confident in his abilities to guide and govern all angelic endeavors with unmatched grace and skill. Every decision he made reflected his notion of unparalleled leadership. In his eyes, not only was he wiser, but also a superior leader. The angels were mere followers, while he possessed the natural gift of command. It was his destiny to guide them all.

Not content with his already lofty status, Lucifer boasted an extraordinary musical talent. None could compare to his enchanting melodies and celestial voice. His performances, resonating through the heavens, captivated all who listened. With an unparalleled ability to play instruments and an incomparable voice, he believed himself to be the supreme musician and vocalist of all creation.

Lucifer treaded upon the holy mount of God, traversing the sacred terrain adorned with stones of fire. His feet touched the divine ground with a sureness that further fueled his pride. These hallowed grounds were his domain, a testament to his exaltation and his unyielding belief in his own unrivaled splendor.

Feelings:

As Lucifer thought on these things within his heart, and continued to gaze upon his beauty in the still water, gradually, he started envision himself as equal with the Almighty God, his Creator, yearning not just for angelic stature, but desiring the title of god of knowledge, instead of "the anointed Cherub. In his quest for godhood, his ambitions took a dark turn.

Yahweh, who had bestowed upon him the gift of nine sacred stones imbued with divine qualities, watched in sorrow as the light within Lucifer dimmed. The stones, once radiant, morphed into nine ominous black stones symbolizing the corruption that consumed him. Each stone represented a vice that Lucifer embraced: pride, perverseness, wickedness, dishonesty, wrongness, injustice, unrighteousness, depravity, and distortion.

Behavior:

As Lucifer stood before Yahweh, a subtle shift in his behavior began to unfold. Once radiant, his celestial light had dimmed, casting a softer glow upon his countenance. And when he raised his voice in song, it was no longer the resounding chorus that had once captivated the heavens. There was a noticeable decrease in its power and conviction.

Gazing upon the face of God became a challenge for Lucifer, for a seed of envy had taken root within him. No longer did he look upon Yahweh with pure admiration and reverence. Instead, there was a longing in his eyes, a desire to possess the glory that he believed should be rightfully shared with him.

And as his gaze wandered, it inevitably fell upon the magnificent throne that Yahweh occupied. However, instead of finding inspiration or awe, Lucifer was filled with envy. The sight of that majestic seat of power stirred within him a burning desire, fueling a deep-seated discontentment that threatened to consume his very soul.

Secret Meetings & Sowing Discord:

First, Lucifer called a secret meeting, those who were under his command did he speak with them first. And said to them, I have assembled you here, to ask you this question, *"Did God really say that He is the only God, and besides Him, there is none other?* [**Isaiah 43:10**]. They replied, *"For Yahweh has declared, "You are my witnesses and servants, that you may know and believe Me, and understand that I am He: before Me there was no God formed, neither shall there be after Me."*

Lucifer replied, *"You have greatly misunderstood His words. But listen to me and I will make His words clear unto you now. For Yahweh didn't really mean that you all could not be gods like Him* [**John 10:34**]. *I have spent more time with Him than you all, and He has made known to me, secret knowledge that has been kept from all except for me. Therefore, a secret knowledge was revealed to me, knowledge that will transform you from a mere angel, into a god like Him."*

With his silver tongue, he whispered to his celestial brethren that he alone possessed a profound, secret knowledge—knowledge capable of elevating them from lowly angels to divine beings.

Lucifer cunningly deceived the angels, weaving a tale of extraordinary power and enticing promises, just like the lies that were told to Eve in the garden. With a sly smile and a persuasive voice, he whispered enticing promises of a secret knowledge that would elevate the angels into godlike beings. He claimed sole possession of this treasured information, proclaiming that only he had the power to unlock their true potential. The allure of godhood gripped their hearts as he vowed to impart this concealed wisdom, but a condition loomed. Proclaiming himself worthy of adoration and exaltation, Lucifer demanded unwavering worship from those who sought to partake in his coveted enlightenment.

"Glorify and worship me, as you do Yahweh," he proclaimed, "and I shall bestow upon you the secrets that will set you above all others. Then, in a moment of time, he showed them galaxies and promised them, "All who bow down and worship me, will I give unto you [**Matthew 4:8-9**] these galaxies, and those angels who worship me not, shall be your servants. They will forever remain beneath us, watching enviously as we ascend." Blinded by desire for divine authority, the angels contemplated their choices, deluded by the temptation of Lucifer's seductive proposition."

As his words echoed through the ethereal realm, curiosity and temptation overpowered some of the unsuspecting angels. Intrigued by Lucifer's tantalizing proposition, they began to question their own divine purpose and entertain the notion of a higher existence. Blinded by ambition and longing for power, they gradually succumbed to Lucifer's deceitful influence.

Little did they know, Lucifer's sweet promises were veiled in treachery, leading them along a dark path of betrayal and downfall. The once united angels now found themselves divided, the fabric of their celestial home unraveling at the seams.

Mystery Revealed: In ***Revelation 12:4*** informs us that the Dragon's tail drew one-third of the angelic beings; which is very important, but why? **Isaiah 9:15** says, "*…and the prophet who teaches falsehood is the tail.*" These two bible verses let me know that Lucifer was prophesying lies unto the angelic beings; speaking to them as if Yahweh was talking through him, but God wasn't. All of the lies came directly from his lying heart.

Matthew 24:4-5 warns us to be watchful, so that no person deceives us, for many will come in Yeshua's name, claiming to be the messiah, and will mislead many. Now, back to the story.

Those angels who succumb to his pernicious rhetoric, and did bow themselves down and worshipped him, as they would Yahweh, and when they bowed themselves down and did worship; the glory of Yahweh that was upon them, lifted off while they were still prostrating before Lucifer. And when they arose, the glory of the Lord God had departed, and their appearance did change to a palish white color.

Once covered by the glorious light of God Himself, now, they looked palish white and somewhat dried. They looked upon themselves and knew right-away, that God's glory was no longer upon them, and neither would it return unto them again. Their eyes did come open and they saw that shame was upon them for all eternity.

When Lucifer saw that the glory of Yahweh had departed from them, a hideous smile came upon his face, for he knew then, that they, like himself, could never be accepted again by Yahweh.

Lucifer said to those who worshipped him, "*My knowledge of good and evil has freed you from the prison of Yahweh. Now, you can make your own choices, whether to obey or disobey Him. But with me, you must obey, so that I may bless you with more secret knowledge and power.*"

From Lucifer's heart, he taught them how to rebel against the Almighty one, for his words were engulf with witchcraft. An addition, he taught them the way of the nine black stones that came from his own heart, and how to used them against other angels. Lucifer instructed his angels, "Continue to present yourselves before Yahweh, for our time to confront the Holy One is not yet." And they obeyed his orders.

He tried to conceal what was in his mind/heart from the Creator by still praising and playing music before Him, but he knew that he could not continual with his shenanigan very long; he had to make his move soon or else be exposed by the Creator. Lucifer and his angels believed that what they had did, was hidden from the Lord God.

Shortly afterward, Lucifer felt something growing inside him, something unlike he had ever felt before, something that felt like a fire burning inside that was consuming him from within [**Ezekiel 28:18**].

He felt like he was giving birth to something that was extremely hostile toward the Creator; something that wasn't subject to Yahweh nor to His will [**Romans 8:7-8**]. Instead of him fighting against this eerie feeling, he submitted himself completely to it; and though he is a spirit, he could feel death within his heart [**Romans 6:23**], but the death that he began to experience was not physical, but spiritual. He knew that he was forever disconnected from Yahweh, and he loved and embraced that feeling.

Soon, Lucifer's propaganda spread throughout the heavens, convincing one-third of the angelic beings to accept his offer [**Revelation 12:3-4**]. During Lucifer's mutiny against Yahweh, The Almighty One didn't confront the wicked one, nor those who joined him, but allow them to continue [**Matthew 13:27-30**] as before; as if He was unaware of their plot.

Gabriel Had Something To Say:

Then Gabriel came before He who lives forever and ever and said, *"My King and Maker, permit your loyal and faithful servant to speak, and I will."* Speak, said the Almighty the Most Holy One! *"Lucifer, along with one-third of your angels, are spreading evil rumors about you, and he is attempting to be your equal, Oh Great and Mighty One. Shall we gather those who have pledge their allegiances to Lucifer and cast them out for their treason, my King?"*

Then said the Creator unto the angel, *"No, but let them be for now* [**Matthew 13:27-30**] *and on a day of My choosing, I will separate the good from the evil, then will they be expelled. Before the thought entered into Lucifer's heart, I knew it.* "There is no darkness, nor shadow of death, where the workers of iniquity may hide themselves from Me, [**Job 34:22**].

Moreover, said He, *"My eyes are in every place, seeing the evil and good,"* [**Proverbs 15:3**]: *but hold your peace and say nothing more on this matter, for all those who believe Me shall not believe him, for they have heard My voice* [**John 10:5**] *and they shall not follow after that deceiver."*

Lucifer's False Belief:

Lucifer believed that the Throne of Yahweh empowered Him to bear rule over the kingdoms of the worlds; for he saw the lightning, thundering, and voices [**Revelation 4:5**] coming out of Yahweh's throne and thought that he should have his own as well, then every angel, those who had already submitted themselves to him, and the ones who rejected his offer, would accept him as being equal with the Creator Himself. Then Lucifer said to those who pledged their allegiances to him:

Lucifer, the fallen angel, held a profound belief that Yahweh's throne stood as the sole obstacle preventing him from attaining parity with the Almighty. With unwavering determination, he fostered a grand scheme in his heart, a prideful declaration echoed in his thoughts: "I will ascend into heaven, exalting my throne above the stars of God. I will sit on the mount of the congregation, on the sides of the north. Ascending above the heights of the clouds, I shall resemble the Most-High."

This audacious proclamation illuminated Lucifer's burning desire to attain supremacy, yearning to surpass the divine limits placed upon him. The allure of Yahweh's celestial dominion became an obsession for Lucifer, propelling him to envision a future where he would stand as an equal to the Almighty, assuming his rightful place beside the heavenly throne.

Prepared For Battle:

Lucifer meticulously crafted his battle plans, driven by a burning ambition to confront Yahweh himself. Gathering one-third of the angels he had cunningly deceived; he sought their allegiance to help him in his audacious fight against Michael and his faithful followers.

His grand vision was to confront Yahweh directly, believing that if he could make Him see reason, they could share heaven as equals. Fueled by his desire to reign supreme, Lucifer planned to establish his dominion on the coveted sides of the north.

Yet, there was a glimmer of hope for a peaceful resolution. Knowing the magnitude of the impending clash, Lucifer considered giving Yahweh an ultimatum - if God didn't agree, war would become inevitable. Secretly hoping that his demands would be met, he hoped to avoid the catastrophic consequences that a celestial war would bring.

Lucifer's battle plans were a blend of strategic prowess and unwavering determination, as he prepared to face off against the mighty forces of Michael and his angels, all with the grand aim of shaping the very heavens themselves.

Mystery Revealed: The reason Yahweh chose "Michael" to fight against Lucifer/Dragon, because his name means: ***"Who Is Like God?"*** Ergo, when Yahweh sent Michael to fight against the dragon, He was sending Lucifer and his angels a strong message: <u>Who Is Like Me</u>, and the answer is; NOBODY!

War In Second Heaven:

In a bold pursuit to confront Yahweh with audacious demands, Lucifer and his angels journeyed towards the divine throne room. Their intention was to negotiate new terms, envisioning a future where Lucifer would stand as an equal to the Almighty and establish his kingdom in the far reaches of the north. However, their quest for power was met with resolute opposition.

With unwavering determination, Michael and his loyal angels intercepted Lucifer and his rebellious cohort, barring their entry to the sacred space. It was undeniable that Yahweh would never accept their audacious terms. The confrontation between heavenly forces ensued, resulting in a crushing defeat for the insubordinate angels, **Revelation 12:7-9**.

As the celestial battle reached its climax, the fallen angels realized the consequences of their defiance. They were soon to face the dire fate of expulsion from the heavenly abode they once called home. Their grand aspirations shattered, Lucifer and his followers were left to ponder the profound cost of their rebellion against the divine order.

Lucifer/Hêlēl And His Angels Are Facing Judgment:

After Lucifer and his angels suffered a horrific defeat, they were forced to stand in the presence of Yahweh and the heavenly host, awaiting judgment for their high crimes. In a thunderous voice, Yahweh charged Lucifer and his angels with the crime of folly [**Joe/Job 4:18**], exposing their reckless rebellion against divine authority. The heavens themselves trembled at the weight of their offenses.

Searing with shame, Lucifer and his angelic followers could only watch as they were subjected to utmost disgrace before the gathered heavenly hosts.

Knowing the severity of their transgressions and iniquities, they were swiftly cast down to the earth with lightning speed, forever separated from their rightful place in the heavens [**Luke 10:18**]. The impact of their fall echoed throughout creation, a testament to the consequences of their defiance.

Thus, Lucifer and his angels, now banished from paradise, would walk the earthly realm, stripped of their former glory and condemned to face the consequences of their high crimes for eternity, **Revelation 12:9**.

Important Intel: Could Lucifer be forgiving if he would have come to Yahweh and repented?
Answer: NO. Here are the five reasons why Yahweh wouldn't have forgiven Lucifer.

Reason One: Lucifer's sin took place in heaven, which deals with eternity. And in eternity, the past, present, and future doesn't exist; only the now is! When Adam and Eve sinned, it occurred in time and therefore, because it happened in time, Yahweh could open the window of time and send His beloved Son, to come and die for our sins.

Reason Two: When Lucifer sinned, no one tempted him; he did it willingly.

Reason Three: Lucifer brought his iniquities into the lives of angels, causing one-third of the heavenly hosts to turn against Yahweh.

Reason Four: While claiming that he wanted to be equal with Yahweh, which was blasphemous, had he achieved his goal, his next step would have been is to completely dethrone the Lord God. He would have had Yahweh to bow down and to worship him.

Reason Five: He didn't believe he was wrong for his transgressions, but rather Yahweh and the angels who choose not to follow him, are the wrong ones.

Satan's Characteristics Through: Animals, Amphibians, and Insects

Here are the animals, amphibians, and insects in the bible that all referred or linked to the devil:
- Old Serpent [Revelation 12:9]
- As a roaring Lion [1st Peter 5:8]
- Wolf [John 7:15, 10:12]
- Defile Bird [Matthew 13:4]
- Great Dragon [Revelation 12:9; 20:2]
- Frogs [Revelation 16:13]
- Flies [Matthew 12:27]

So, now that we are aware of the animals, amphibians, and insects that reveal something about Satan's personalities, lets understand these better:

Serpents/Snakes: There are three different kinds of snakes: Constrictors, Venomous, and Poisonous.
Constrictor snakes, such as python and anaconda, grabs its prey with its teeth, then quickly wraps coils of its body around the prey and squeezes. Whenever their prey attempts to exhale, the snake will squeeze tighter. And once the animal's heart stops beating, the snake advances to the prey's head and begin swollen it whole.

Satan's Personality Seen Through Constrictor Snakes: Whenever a person feels like life is being squeezed out of them, or people is draining their energy or life-force, it's because the demon with the characteristics of a python or anaconda is attacking him or her. But this isn't the kind of squeeze of a person who's under temporary pressure, but rather constant force being applied to their life, nonstop!

Information: Oftentimes, Satan uses people to squeeze the life out of others, making life much harder than it has to be.
A sign that a demon is using a certain person against you or a loved one. All constrictor snakes, tighten their grip upon their prey, only when the animal being squeezed, attempts to exhale; and this can be said about a person who is either oppressed by, or possessed with demons, he or she isn't able to forgive others, or to let go of the hurt they have endured, while they themselves, desire for others to forgive them.

And whenever the person tries to forgive, demons immediately bring back the hurtful memories and words that were said and done to them, so, is to prevent them from forgiving.

But if that individual continues to accept the mental images and voices from the demons, they are likely to share their unforgiving messages to the very ones they claim to love, which will cause their loved ones to develop hatred within their heart as well.

Please keep in mind that demons are uncapable of forgiving anyone. They are full of hate and bitterness, only a person who has true love in their heart, can forgive someone who doesn't deserve forgiveness.

Something to think about: I know some Christians, who are able to speak in tongues [one of the gifts of the Holy Spirit], but unable to speak in the language of love and forgiveness. **Important Intel**: While a person can fake a spiritual gift, he or she can't fake the fruits of the Holy Spirit. This is why Yeshua said, *"You shall know them by their fruits,"* [**Matthew 7:15-20**].

Something to think about: The last prayer that Yeshua prayed for those who mocked Him, while dying on the cross was this, *"Father, forgive them, for they don't know what they're doing,"* **Luke 23:34**. Now, if He could forgive those who advocated for his death and mocked Him as He was dying, how is it that you cannot forgive someone else?

Forgiveness isn't something that frees the offender, but rather it's a gift that liberates the person who's doing the forgiving. As long as the person isn't willing to forgive the person or persons who hurt them, they become a victim, constantly thinking about who that person hurt you, what they said, what they did or didn't do, and so on. What a nightmare, each day, filled with hurt and sorrows!

Two Kinds of Forgiveness: There are two kinds of forgiveness, one is for yourself and the other one, is for something other than yourself. You would be surprise of the people who hasn't forgiven themselves for their past mistakes. You made a mistake, okay, now it's time to forgive yourself. For the exception of Yeshua, everyone in this world or, who has ever lived, has made mistakes; not just little ones, but big ones, you just don't know about them.

The bible says that we all have sinned and come short of the glory of God, **Romans 3:23**. Later, I will explain why demons are doing everything within their powers, is to prevent a person from forgiving, whether it is their self or someone else.

Important Information: Everything needs to eat, or else, it will soon die; this includes demonic spirits, they need to eat off of a person's hurts, suffering, and pain, and when a person refuses to feed them, while they will not die physically, nevertheless, they will die from governing over that person's life.

Important Information: No Christian can be possessed by a demon, but they can be oppressed by one.

Here is an exercise for those of you who desire to stop the demonic spirit of the constrictor, to loosen its grip over your life and eventually, stopping it from destroying you.

Venomous snakes, such as cobras, rattlers, and so on, kill their prey by biting and ejecting saliva, toxins.

Satan's Personality Seen Through Venomous Snakes: Just as a venomous snake venom is poisonous to its prey, Satan uses the tongue/words of other to inflict devastating wounds upon the hearts and lives of others. Oftentimes, it's in the form of gossiping, such as divulging someone else's shameful past mistakes, so everyone can know about it. Satan uses these gaslighted insidious words and behaviors is to unleash his wicked kingdom into their lives, and the lives of their descendants.

Information: Oftentimes, demons work through certain people's words in order to mislead or to dupe others, just as the serpent used its grandiloquence speech to beguile Eve in the Bible. These kinds of people might appear to be innocent and noble at first, appearing to be helpful and offering good advice, in order to weakening or to lower their victim's defenses, but after a few hours or days of listening to them, their words will become insidious and their pernicious motives and heart will be manifested.

No offense, but the vast of politician's words are influenced and based on Satan's lies, telling their victims, I mean voters, things that want to hear and do, but their ears and heart is only available for their rich donors and special interests.

Poisonous snakes: While a venomous snake can be eaten, a poisonous snake cannot because its skin has poison within it. If a human touch it skin, the poison will enter his or her skin and can kill them.

Satan's Personality Seen Through A Poisonous Snake: With some people, the moment you get involved with them, you start to go down in life and everything else. This is because that person's entire life is toxic or

poisonous, and if you connect with them, get ready to lose whatsoever is valuable to you. Oftentimes, these kinds of persons are abusive in some form or another: verbal, physical, mental, and or sexual.
Think about all those who has listened to Satan, what has been their outcome? Whether it was the angels in heaven or, Adam and Eve! Everything with and about Satan is toxic and harmful, because that is who he is!

Overview Of Serpents: Snakes are low to the ground, making them inconspicuous unless they want to be seen. Whenever they're moving, nothing but silence can be heard. There surrounding are their coverings or camouflage.

When they hunt for food, stealth and quietness are their allies until they are ready to ambush an animal, and when striking at their target, lightning is their friend.

Whenever they are killing their victim, silence can only be heard from them. While swallowing their victim whole, no growling, like the lion, and whenever they're finished consuming their food, nothing is left behind; no evidence can be collected that another animal had been there.
And when the snake leaves that area, they do so in silence, just like they came.

One Character of Demons: Whenever demons are planning to attack a person, first of all, they will do so in silence. But their silence is linked to that person's ignorance of the devil's tricks; in other words, demons are counting on their victim's lack of knowledge and awareness of their wicked schemes, and that is how they move in silence.

Most people, including many Christians, are unaware that many times, their environment is a perfect camouflage for demons to remain inconspicuous. For instance, demons are able to hide in their music, songs that either glorifies the listener or, the singer is glorifying them own-self.

Movies that not only blasphemy the name of God, in which many proclaim that He's their God, but also promotes adultery, fornication, witchcraft, and other works of the flesh.

Final Comment: Satan is known as the "*Old Serpent*" because he doesn't have any new tricks, neither does he need them, because his same old ones have been working well, since he was in eternity and in this present day.

So, he doesn't have a reason to change his methods; please keep this in mind.

Roaring Lions: The Bible says that Satan comes as a roaring lion, seeking in whom he can destroy [1ˢᵗ **Peter 5:8**]; so then, that being said, let's examine the behavior of lions and by doing so, we can see how Satan works and demons plans for taking you and your family down.

Stalking Prey: Lions, the majestic predators of the wild, have perfected the art of stalking. Their hunting technique combines stealth, patience, and extraordinary agility. When lions spot their prey, they switch into stealth mode, lowering their muscular bodies, ready to pounce at any given moment.

Using the surrounding vegetation and terrain to their advantage, lions move cautiously and silently, making every step calculated. Their powerful legs enable them to move swiftly, while their keen eyesight aids them in keeping track of their quarry. With each gradual movement, they mimic the presence of a shadow, blending seamlessly into their hunting grounds.

Lions utilize teamwork to increase their chances of success, often employing the element of surprise. Some members of the pride take up flanking positions, while others advance from the front. This strategic positioning ensures that their prey is surrounded, minimizing the chances of escape.

Once the lion makes his move, it is an awe-inspiring display of speed and strength. In one swift bound, he lunges towards his target, closing the gap with astonishing precision. The final moments of the stalk erupt into a relentless pursuit, as the lion unleashes its raw power to bring down its prey.
In the savannah, witnessing a lion stalking its prey is a testament to nature's awe-inspiring beauty and the predator's remarkable hunting prowess.

But for those who are familiar with the behavior of lions, know that they will not launch an attack, without first, studying the herd of animals, identifying the young, weak, and eldest, in order to catch an easy meal. And when it has all the information needed, other lions will help and setting up the ambush.

Rewrite: In order to help you understand demons, I will be rewriting this, instead of using lions, I will be using the word "Demons," to make better sense of their operations.

Demons, the majestic predators in the world today, have perfected the art of stalking you and your loved ones. Their hunting technique combines stealth, patience, and extraordinary agility. When your mother decided not to abort you and you entered out of her womb, demons immediately identify you as their prey, they switch into stealth mode by trying to cause you to doubt that you were made in God's image and likeliness, you're more than a conquer in Christ Jesus, and that you are a child of the Most-High God, and once they have persuaded you, they can pounce at any given moment.

Using your past mistakes, people's negative views of you, and your current sufferings to their advantage, demons move cautiously and silently, making every step calculated, and hoping that you don't notice them until they have fully executed their plans for your life. Your lack of knowledge of them have enable them to move swiftly, while their keen eyesight aids them in keeping track of their quarry.
With each gradual movement, they mimic the presence of a shadow, blending seamlessly into their hunting grounds.

Demons utilize teamwork to increase their chances of success, often employing the element of surprise. Some members of the pride take up flanking positions, while others advance from the front. This strategic positioning ensures that they have surrounded you, minimizing the chances of escape.

Once a demon makes its move, it is an awe-inspiring display of speed and strength. In one swift bound, it will lunge towards you, closing the gap with astonishing precision. The final moments of the stalk erupt into a relentless pursuit, as the demons unleashes their raw power to bring you down.

In this day and age, witnessing demons stalking humans, using their same old deceptive tricks, is a testament to nature's awe-disturbing wickedness and the predator's remarkable hunting prowess.

Chase Me: While watching a lioness on television one day, I saw her approaching its prey as it was drinking water. That animal quickly turned around and identified the lioness. Once the lioness knew her cover had been blown, she permitted that same animal to chase her, as if the lioness was now afraid; but this sudden turn of event was all a part of the lioness plan, knowing that the animal would pursue her, she could lead the animal were the lionesses were lurking. And when the prey arrived at the other lionesses' location, all of them came out and surrounded that animal and immediately killed and ate it.

Rewrite: Demons love to attack a person when they're not watching, praying, studying their bible, connecting with other saints, and so on. But when that individual becomes aware that a demon is ready to attack him or her, it may appear to back off, even appearing to be afraid and permit that person to chase it, so that person can go out and start ministering the gospel and begin attacking the kingdom of darkness, even though, that person hasn't repented of their current sins, not studying their bible, and hasn't forgiving others.

Then, that demon will let that person have some success and may appear to be winning, and then, lead it into an ambush, where they will tempt to kill that person's reputation, character, and good works.

My point is, before demons attack a person, they study that individual for a while, learning his or her patterns, their prayer life, fasting, spiritual walk with Yahweh, how many other people is willing to help them fight if they attack that individual, and so on, and then come with the element of surprise.

Bring Down Prey: By surrounding the prey, they create a wall of intimidating force, increasing their chances of success. While some lions distract and provoke the prey, others take advantage of the moment and make the final, decisive move to bring it down.

The lions' sharp retractable claws and strong jaws come into play, as they aim to immobilize the prey by going for the throat or suffocating it. The sheer force of their weight and muscles allows them to overpower even larger and more formidable animals. One lion will bite on the animal's rear leg, near its stomach, one will jump upon its back and bite its spine, and the third one will either bite its throat or, use its mouth to cover the animal's nose, in attempt to suffocate it.

Once the prey is successfully brought down, the pride works in unison to ensure a fair share of the hard-earned meal.

Rewrite: By surrounding the person with problems, guilt, shame, and their haters, demons create a wall of intimidating force, increasing their chances of causing the person to destroy their own life, or the life of someone else. While some demons like to distract their victims with false entertainment, drugs, and or alcohol, other try to provoke them to hate and blame God for all of their pain, in order to take advantage of the moment and make the final, decisive move to bring him or her down.

The demons subtle and insidious rhetoric comes into play, as they aim to immobilize the person by going for the things that are most precious to that individual. The sheer force of their weighed lies and evil influences allows them to overpower anyone who's not cover by the precious blood of Jesus.

One demon will attack the person's walk with Yahweh, while the other one will attack their faith in Him, and the final demon will attempt to destroy the individual's life.
Once the person has been successfully brought down, the demons work in unison to ensure that the person remain down, until they die.

Wolves: They are highly intelligent animals and very social, developing close bonds with family members and their pack. Gray wolves in the wild oftentimes show significant displays of affection and other emotions with each other.

Once a wolf has found their mate, they tend to remain with each other until death do them apart. Wolves are known to die for one another, this reveals the closest of their bond.
And while they are not known for having great speed, they are good marathon endurance runners; so, they don't have to be the fastest, they know that while the other animal might outrun them, their endurance will pay off.

Rewrite: Demons are highly intelligent spiritual beings and love to work in cohesion. Once a demon has found a person who's willing to tolerate its wicked behavior, it tends to remain with that person, even believing that that person is their house for it to live. While they know that the person may be able to void them for a while, all it needs to do is be patient, for it knows that the person will soon become spiritual tired, becoming weary in well doing, and it can reenter the individual again, but next time, bring in additional evil spirits.

Special Information: If a person was in a jungle, evergreen forests, are any other place where dangerous animals roam, and suddenly silence surrounds them, then he or she should be on guard because a predator is nearby. By watching the behaviors of the people in that area or region, if you notice a sudden silence or agitation among them, then you need to become watchful.
This method can be used to know when he or she will be attacked by a demon(s). For the average Christian, he or she can expect four major fights from demons each year. But how do I know this? Let's read "**Luke 4:13**," *"And when the devil had ended all the temptation, he departed from Him for a season."*

Defile Birds: While such birds as the buzzards, kites, vultures, eagles, and so on, eat rotten flesh, I will use the raven birds to represent the foul birds or demons for two reasons. *Reason one*: This was the first bird that Noah sent out, when he wanted to know had the waters began to recede from of the face of the earth [**Genesis 8:1**]. *Reason two*, they are known for their intelligence.

"And as he sowed, some seeds fell along the path, and the birds came and devoured them," **Matthew 13:4 ESV**. Later, the bible reveal that the seed represent the word of God and the fowls of the air, represent demons. Whenever the word of God is preached or taught, demons will be present, is to stop the people from understanding it.

Special Comment: This is why, before the church service begins, that the person opening up the service should pray over the congregation, and in Jesus' name, binding the raven's spirit, preventing it from being able to steal the words that is being preached or taught during church service.

So, then how do these evil spirits hinder the person from understanding what is being taught? Remember, the ravens enjoy eating on dead things, therefore, while in service, the demons will bring something hurtful, embarrassing, or troublesome to that individual's mind, causing their focus to dwell on it, instead of on the solution, which is on Jesus Christ.

Ravens will kill its prey also. The demons will wait until you're in the spirit, and then have someone to bother you, or have your child to misbehave, right when you were about to receive your breakthrough, all in attempt to kill your joy.

True Story: I walked into the church that day with a heavy burden weighing me down. As I sat there, desperately seeking a breakthrough, a glimmer of hope started to shine through the darkness, as the choir was singing praises unto Yahweh. I got up for my seat and begin praising my Lord God with all of my heart and afterwards, my heavy burdens begin to lift. But then, in the midst of my praise, someone approached me and chose to interrupt the sacred moment. I couldn't help but wonder why they couldn't have chosen another spot to sit, for it seemed like an intentional act to sabotage my divine connection. It felt as if Satan himself had sent this person to stop my breakthrough.

With my moment of triumph abruptly halted, the devil wasted no time in reminding me of my problems. The shame washed over me, discouraging my spirit and causing me to question my very presence in the church service. My initial motivation was replaced by a desire to escape, to leave this place where my breakthrough was shattered and my vulnerability exploited. I couldn't even focus as the minister taught the word, due to the woman's children misbehaving during the service.

Later, it was revealed to me that Satan doesn't care who he can use, as so long as he can hinder or stop someone from getting their breakthrough.

In conclusion: The foul spirit job is to prevent the person from understanding and holding on to the words of Yeshua.

Dragon: "His tail [Lucifer/Satan] swept down a third of the stars [angels] of heaven and cast them to the earth. And the dragon stood before the woman who was about to give birth, so that when she bore her child he might devour it," **Revelation 12:4 ESV**. Whenever the bible is referring to Satan as the dragon, it is due to his ability to draw those who once walked with and served God, but turned from Him, in order to follow after a liar, and to fight against the woman, which represented the church.

The dragon waited until the woman was physically weak, ready to give birth, and after giving birth, planned to attack and kill her child.
It is so important for the saints to protect the young or immature Christians in church, because if not, most likely, Satan is going to destroy their relationship with Yahweh. Let's look at the dragon's tail for a moment, *"And the prophet who teaches lies is the tail,"* **Isaiah 9:15**.

Flies: House flies are a nasty insect. They feed on fecal matter, discharges from open wounds and sores, sputum, and moist decaying organic matter. They will eat from garbage, sewers, rotting meats, the carcasses of animals and humans. Flies eat through regurgitation; this is how they soften their food and eat. When a fly lands on your favorite picnic fare, it throws up a little, softening up the food and eating its fill. Then it flies away, leaving the rest of your food on the table.

They carry millions of germs and diseases, and as a result, causing many illnesses. After landing on the most disgusting things, they will fly and land on your mouth, food, drink, sore, and etc.
They are fast breeders; a single pair can produce thousands of maggots in a surprisingly short period of time. Even their buzzing is extremely alarming to our ears.

Demon's words and behaviors, should be as appalling as flies. Whenever they try to talk to you, it should sound like the buzzing of flies to your ears. Whenever they try to enter your home, you should immediately eliminate them with the word of God, because you know once in, they're going to make everyone in your home ill, bring in their sicken lies. If you don't cast them out of your home, then the same diseases of hatred and foolishness, that got them thrown out of heaven, will they bring to your house.

The same lies they used to get someone's else child murdered, they want to share it with your children, so they too, can be slaughtered. The same lies they told to some young men, that they should enter a public school with many guns, and take as many lives as possible, and afterwards, take that same weapon and blow their own brains out, the demons want to teach it to your sons.

The same lies they told to the young girls, convincing them that the only way to get ahead in life, making a lot of money and gain popularity, is to use their beauty to make only fans and or, pornography movies, this same toxic message, is what they're going to teach to your daughters, so they too can become whores, if you let them into your home. In addition, they will teach your daughters the lies that all men are no good. The same lies that they have used to cause billions of people to enter into hell of fire, and soon, into the lake of fire, they want to teach it to your children, if you let them.

Q. I have a serious question for you [the reader]? Would you invite this kind of person into your home? Imagine encountering someone who not only lies but they are the creator of all lies and deceptions, in fact, the foundation of their native language is based on lies. This person has a special relation with lies, to the point, he's, their father.

This individual isn't content with dishonesty alone; and every deal that he has ever made with someone, whether with angelic beings are with humans, has being to his advantage, but their downfall. He's the one who whispered into the ears of those who entered into schools with multiple firearms, and told them that if they kill as many innocent people as possible, then they would become a legend; forever be known as a hero. Then afterward the mass shooting, he tells the shooter, "_Now that's you're a hero, put the gun to your head and pull the trigger. Don't let them take you alive_!"

His sole mission in life is surrounded by stealing, killing, and destroying the lives of others. He wants to steal your marriage, friendships, funds, and anything else he can get his hands on. Whenever he learns about your dreams in life, immediately he begins working on how to destroy them. This person is the one who directs a terrorist where to go, where there will be the most people available, and then to cry out "Allahu Akbar" before detonating the bomb that was strapped across their body.

But that's not all. This person derives satisfaction from manipulating others into making mistakes, only to turn around and accuse them before Yahweh.
Worse yet, they are the puppeteer behind every sinful act, lurking in the shadows as the orchestrator of all that is rotten. Every negative thing that you're hearing about on your local or cable news, he's behind it.

He's the caused of every overdose case. He's the inner voice that tells a man, "_Go and beat your woman, that will make her start listening to you!_" He's the voice that tells a man, "When you leave the woman, the children are no longer your responsibility." He's the voice that causes a person to abide in their mistakes. He is behind every war and genocide and so on.

Now, would you allow this kind of person into your home?

Would you permit him to be alone with your children, or to teach them? Before you say, no, is he already in your home, not only talking with you, but raising your children?

I have just described a little of Satan's character.

Secret Worship:

Yoga: While most people do Yaga for health benefits, but what they don't know it that its demon worship. It is a Hindu practice. It is a spiritual worship of Hindu gods, using physical ascenders or poses, to pay homage to their many gods. Ergo, it is a spiritual practice with physical benefits; not the other way around. A person cannot separate the spiritual aspects from the physically, because they're in oneness.

Even if a person's intentions are pure, that doesn't matter with demons. The devil doesn't care because the person is ignorant about what they're doing, as long as it receives the glory.

You see, whether the person worship Satan by attending some satanic ritual or going to their yoga class, as long as they can receive the praises, that's all that matters to them.

Amapiano dance (South Africa dance) is another form of demonic worship. As the person performs the moments, their eyes begin rolling backwards into their head, an upward gaze, is known to activate and stimulate intuition and higher consciousness, connecting with their ancestry, which is nothing more than linking them with familiar spirits.
The bible strictly forbids the living, trying to communicate with the dead [**Deuteronomy 18:10-12**].

CASE TWO: *Demons With Human-Like Personalities*

Demons are more than just ethereal spirits; they possess human-like personalities, which makes them remarkably adept at both connecting with people and deceiving them effortlessly. Understanding their nature means recognizing the signs of their demonic personality. One hallmark of their presence is witnessing their amusement at others' misfortune. For instance, when a demon enters a person, he or she takes on that evil spirit's sense of humor, attitude, mission, and or mindset.

Better Understanding: In **Revelation 13:1**, John saw a beast {antichrist} risen up out of the sea {people}, but why is this relevant? Though the antichrist is led by Satan himself, he will be able to relate to the people in that era, unlike any other human, knowing exactly how they're feeling and will give them temporary relief from their suffering. He will be the hero that this world has being longing for. Solving complex problems, even making a way for Israel and the Palestinians to have a two-state solution, which will end in a catastrophe. *Only the antichrist and false prophet will be allowed to make the deal with Israel and the Palestinians.*

Ultimately, demons harbor an offensive hatred towards God, directing their animosity with all their hearts. Their fervent desire is to alter the image of humans, ensuring that they no longer resemble the divine reflection of God but rather mirror the likeness of demons themselves. Lurking within the ethereal realm of spirits, they manifest solely through the havoc and turmoil they create.
Thus, demons are resolute in their determination to persuade humans to think, feel, and act in accordance with their own sinister nature. Their intention is to taint the purity and goodness bestowed upon humanity by God, leading individuals away from righteousness and towards malevolence. Such is the motivation behind the manipulative actions instigated by demons—maneuvering society towards a distorted reflection, steering it away from its inherently godly roots.

Demonic Sense of Humor: Whenever a person opens themselves to this kind of demon, it causes him or her to find it amusing at others mishaps, such as laughing when an individual stumbles down stairs or endures an accidental injury. Instead of being concerned and seeing if that person has broken a limb, and see how can they aid them, if necessary, laughter and enjoyment is immediately revealed. This sadistic pleasure highlights their perverse sense of humor while showcasing their inclination towards schadenfreude.

Moreover, demons exhibit behavioral patterns reminiscent of childish or offensive pranks, causing the person who's under their control to play dangerous pranks that can cause either themselves or, someone else to lose their life, all for laughs and to gain followers for their social media.

They excel at playing tricks on unsuspecting victims, often exploiting their vulnerabilities and deepest fears. It is through these cunning actions that they derive satisfaction and feed on the chaos they create. While attempting to frighten someone, they don't know the condition of the other person's heart, neither do the demon permits them to think about such a thing before doing the prank, no, it just wants others to laugh and to follow them on social media.

Their ability to transform minor nuisances into massive disturbances is a testament to their shrewd intelligence and manipulative ways.
In essence, demons possess a unique blend of spiritual essence and human-

like traits, making them formidable adversaries in their ability to relate, deceive, and exploit our weaknesses.

Here, I will be listing ten common demonic personalities; in other words, demons working through the behavioral of certain people:

The Offensive Jester: This kind of fiend expresses itself through comedy, causing the jester to use inappropriately jokes and or gestures, often crossing boundaries with their dark sense of humor. They delight in making others uncomfortable or upset, reveling in their ability to push people's buttons. All offensive behaviors are on the table, just for laughs.

The Arrogant demon behavior: This demon expresses itself through an individual, causing him or her to project a condescending attitude toward others, believing themselves to be superior in every way. They demean and belittle, feeding off the power they feel when making others feel small or insignificant. The person may use their money, position, or material possessions to berate others who aren't as privilege as themselves.
They can also be overweening due to their good-looks; causing those who aren't as attractive as themselves, to hide in the shadows.

The Bullying type Demon: This demon, when it enters a person, causing him or her to intimidate, use physical violence, and or torment others. These demons cause the person to seek out people who they view as weaker, inferior, or in a position where the person isn't able to fully defend themselves. They derive pleasure from inflicting emotional or physical harm, seeking to dominate and control their victims through fear and aggression.

The Comfortable Victim: Demons express themselves through individuals who choose to remain a victim, causing the person to accept being a slave to other people toxic behaviors, actions, and abuse. One of the first signs of this evil spirit at work, is whenever you see a person who's constantly seeking attention and sympathy from others; whether the attention is negative or positive. They manipulate situations to ensure they are the center of attention, exploiting their perceived misfortunes for their own gain.

These kinds of persons don't really want help, just someone to feel sorry for them. When giving sound and proven advice, they will pretend to take heed, but shortly afterwards, they will be either at your doorstep or calling, and repeating the same old conversation as before.

The Manipulative Puppeteer: This demonic entity works through those who are narcissistic. The person makes everything about themselves, while everyone else is irrelevant. The person must be the center of attention, no exceptions! The demon causes the person to believe that he or she is far more important, than what they really are.

For example: a woman can insist on dating a high-value-man, over six-feet tall in height, handsome, and makes over a hundred-thousand dollars a year. And while it's nothing wrong with desiring such a man; it is wrong to insist on dating such a man when she herself has very little to offer in return.

She could have a child, not making six-figures herself, and once her makeup is removed, isn't very pretty, but maybe average or a little below, and only believes she's a good woman, because she and her friends think so.

The Sex Slave: I'm not referring to the young girl who has been forced into some kind of sex trade, rather those who are doing "Only-Fans, prostitution, escort, porn, etc." demons are expressing themselves through these individuals, deceiving them into believing that that's the only way for them to live out their dreams in life. Through these people, Satan is able to release his demons of adultery {spiritual adultery} into the lives of all those who view such a thing.

Something to think about: What kind of person who is willing to show their private parts for the
entire world to see, unless he or she were under the influence or control of a demon?

The Spirit of Greed: While there isn't anything wrong with having money and wanting more, it is wrong when someone is willing to harm others in order to gain it. When people are controlled by demons, the insidious force of greed tends to rear its ugly head. This becomes evident when examining the actions of pharmaceutical companies, driven more by their desire for massive profits than by the noble intention of making medications affordable for all. Price gouging becomes commonplace, leaving countless individuals struggling to bear the burden of exorbitant prices. It's disheartening to witness such a blatant disregard for the well-being of those in need.

Furthermore, in the United States, our society faces the overwhelming weight of taxation. As our hard-earned money is siphoned away, the harsh reality becomes clearer: we are being taxed to death. It is particularly disconcerting when considering the vast amounts of money pumped into our military, reaching trillions of dollars each year. Meanwhile, on a global scale, countless innocent children suffer and die due to starvation. It is a painful irony that our priorities seem so skewed, focusing on destructive power rather than alleviating the suffering of the most vulnerable.

The rampant presence of greed has insidiously infiltrated our esteemed FDA, leading them to conveniently overlook the insidious influx of noxious substances within our nourishment and beverages. With alarming regularity, the FDA grants approval to companies allowing the incorporation of deleterious food coloring agents that pose grave threats to our well-being. These chemical additives, such as yellow 5 and 6, as well as red 40, have been linked to a host of health complications, that are known cancer-causing substances.

<u>Spirit of Racism</u>: Whenever you come across the ugly presence of racism, it's important to understand that hatred and pride are lurking close by, as they are all interconnected. Demons, some of them, find a way to manifest themselves through racism, using it as a channel to express their wicked nature. These malevolent beings deceive individuals, convincing them that they are superior to certain groups solely based on the color of their skin.

However, it is crucial to remember that racism is not an innate trait; it is a learned behavior. It is unfortunate that some individuals succumb to the influence of these demons, falling into the trap of bigotry and discrimination. But just as racism is taught, it can also be untaught. By fostering empathy, education, and understanding, we can work towards dismantling this toxic belief system and create a more inclusive and accepting society.

So, whenever you encounter racism, be aware that the roots of hatred and pride are intertwined with it. By recognizing and confronting these demons, we can strive for a future where the darkness of racism no longer has a place in our hearts or in our world.

CASE THREE: <u>Satan's False Light</u>

In this section, you will learn about these things:
- Satan's false light
- Satan deceiving through religions

Satan, the ultimate deceiver, cunningly disguises himself as an angel of light, and sadly to say, he has been very successful at convincing billions of people, in heaven and throughout the history of humanity, to believe and accept his deceptive light as truth.

But just how deceptive and alluring is Satan's conning light? In order for us to understand the power and deceptive of his false light, I need to reveal a little more of Yahweh, and in doing so, I think we can understand just how powerful his false light is:

Yahweh, the Almighty, is far too holy for mortal eyes to dare gaze upon. This truth has been revealed through scripture, specifically in **Exodus 33:20**, where it is proclaimed that no human being can behold His face and live. His magnificence exceeds our mere physical forms.

Nevertheless, the book of Revelation grants us a glimpse, albeit limited, into His majestic presence. His head, like pure wool, shines as white as the purest snow. His eyes blaze with an intensity akin to consuming fire, radiating an unfathomable power. His face shines greater than any star. His voice resonates like the roaring tumult of numerous mighty waters, commanding respect and awe. And His feet, resembling glowing bronze from a blazing furnace, symbolize strength and unyielding righteousness.

Yet, as sinful creatures, we are deemed unworthy to truly behold the full glory of God. His appearance is simply too magnificent for our human imperfections to comprehend. Thus, we must humbly acknowledge our limitations and approach the divine with reverence, understanding that our understanding is but a glimpse into the boundless transcendence of God's nature.

Words cannot express God's true holiness and just how wonderful He is. Yahweh, the Almighty, is so holy that even the Seraphim, celestial beings of unparalleled purity, fly around His divine throne, their voices echoing through the heavens. With reverent awe, they proclaim, "Holy, holy, holy is our Lord God."

In their majestic flight, the Seraphim draw closer to the glory of God, beholding Him in all His splendor. Their every wingbeat resounds with the magnitude of His holiness, a symphony of adoration that pierces the celestial realm. And yet, the depths of Yahweh's holiness remain unfathomable, beyond the confines of mortal comprehension.

The Seraphim, with their unwavering devotion, invite us to glimpse the vastness of His perfect nature. They beckon us to lift our voices in praise and join their heavenly chorus. For in the presence of our Lord God, all creation is hushed, overwhelmed by the radiance of His holiness. May we, as His cherished children, forever acknowledge and honor His incomparable majesty.

Now, as holy and wonderful Yahweh is, Lucifer was able to persuade one-third of the angelic beings to exchange Yahweh's light, for his. The angels that Satan misled, didn't have to read a book in order to learn about the awesome creator, or to wait until death in order to behold Him, for they are able to see Him as He truly is.

They didn't have to read about how He made the stars, moons, black holes, comets, universe, and so on, because they were a witness to His mighty powers. They knew that He not only created all of those things, but also had created them; and could testify that besides Him, there was no other god. And yet, Satan/Lucifer convinced one-third of them to pledge their allegiance to him and as a result, to be expelled from heaven and one day, to spend eternity in the lake of fire.

Dream of Mine: Two times did I see the Lord God in dreams. **The First Time:** For years, my deepest desire had been to see Jesus Christ, the embodiment of the incredible sacrifice made for my sins. Then, one night, in the realm of dreams, my prayers were answered. There He was, standing before me, with His comforting arm draped around my beloved mother. It was a moment of awe and wonder.

Jesus' gaze was penetrating; His eyes could see right into the depths of my soul. It was as though I were a transparent glass window, and He could read my every thought before it even formed in my mind. His mouth did not move, yet His words resonated in my being through a form of telepathy. He asked a simple but profound question, "Do you love me?"

In that sacred moment, I instinctively looked at my mother, standing by Jesus' side, and implored her to convey my love for Him. She turned to Him and proclaimed, "Jesus, he loves you." His eyes shifted briefly towards my mother, then focused back on me, and He repeated the question, "Do you love me?"

I took a step back, feeling a mixture of disappointment and sorrow upon waking up. I reached out to God in prayer, expressing my regret for not being able to openly declare my love for the One I had yearned to see. And then, in that still, small voice, He comforted me, reminding me that He sees beyond mere words.
His gaze transcends the surface and penetrates straight into the depths of the heart.

I realized that I could not deceive or hide anything from Him, for His all-knowing presence encompasses every aspect of my being. In His divine wisdom, He chooses to look upon the heart, seeking the truth of our love, rather than relying solely on the words we speak.

From that profound encounter, I gained a deeper understanding of the authenticity that God seeks from His followers. My love for Him must be genuine, emanating from the depths of my soul, for He knows the truth even before it reaches my lips.

His deceptive illusions haven't changed, since his fall from heaven, but has remained consistent, ever since the days of Adam and Eve, causing them to receive his damnable light. Henceforth, humans would suffer from every kind of sickness, disease, death, and billions have lost their soul and spirit in hell of fire.

This false light of Satan, gleams with the allure of goodness and benevolence, drawing individuals closer to the jaws of darkness, spiritual death, and the lake of fire.

The Second Dream of Mine: The second time I beheld my Lord and God appeared in a vivid dream, years after the initial encounter. This time, the dream unfolded in a hospital setting, with Kathy, a woman who had once watched over me in childhood, leading the way. "You said you wanted to see the Lord, so come and see," Kathy's voice echoed as we journeyed through the hospital corridors.

Passing the bustling information desk, my gaze drifted to the waiting room, where patients sought solace, and a trio of medical professionals disembarked from an elevator. Gently guiding me, Kathy pressed the number 4, and we ascended to the fourth floor.

Confusion momentarily clouded my path, so I was headed toward the right, but Kathy redirecting me towards the left. Two looming figures, towering at least ten feet, stood at the entrance, they were talking until they saw us, then they stopped and gazed upon us.

As I peered into the room, a breathtaking sight awaited me. My Lord God, seated upon an immense throne of purest white, radiated a brilliance akin to lightning. His exalted stature, like that of a tornado even in repose, left me awe-struck. Though the divine radiance permitted me only a fleeting glimpse, Kathy gently held my left hand and guided me closer to the throne. My heart raced as we approached, observing countless others standing in reverent queue, their eyes fixed upon us, yet their lips silent. At the throne's threshold, I beheld the raw essence of sheer power, even without glimpsing His countenance. Yahweh didn't just have power; He was the very source of it.

I wasn't allowed to see His face, but rather His image, that was pure light, and that of a man.
Overwhelmed, I spoke to Kathy, my voice trembling with a mix of joy and trepidation. "I know I am dreaming, but if you allow me to look upon God again, I am going to die in my sleep." Instantly, Kathy grasped my right hand, and at the speed of light, we left His divine presence. We went to another part of the dream, but I will not reveal it at this time.

I revealed these two dreams to inform you that, Yahweh is far more awesome than you can ever imagine or think. When I saw Him briefly, I knew that He made all things and they weren't difficult for Him to make. Whatsoever He thought about, it would have immediately come to pass. But when pride and the other eight stone present itself in a person's life, they become as foolish as Lucifer and his demons, thinking that they can be equal with God or can replace Him.

Q. ***How is Satan false light currently bamboozling billions of people in today's world?***
Trying Your Best: His false light deceives people into believing that they're walking in God's righteousness, when in reality, they are walking in real darkness; projecting a form of godliness [**2nd Timothy 3:5**], while denying the power thereof.

Q. How can I know if I am walking in a false light or not?
A. The form of godliness is when a person is able to perform the religious rituals, but the love of God isn't abiding in them. In addition, when the word of God isn't causing them to change for the best. A person should be very alarmed whenever the bible hasn't a positive effect on their lifestyle,

meaning they can sit in church, read their bible, and yet, continue in their sins.

True Story: I was in a men's clothing store, and Easter Sunday was that next following week. While I was shopping for a suit, I overheard a man talking with the salesclerk about how he must out-dress the other deacons that were going to be there on Easter. This deacon entire focus was on his clothing and shoes; not one time did he talk about how he wanted to look good for the Lord God. And sad to say, his wife was cheering him on, talking about how he was going to be better dressed than all of the other deacons.

Easter Sunday wasn't going to be about how he was going to recognized Yeshua and His mighty sacrifices and how he was going to be praying for those who might come to the alter and repent, but rather about how good he was going to look on that Sunday. This man was being blinded by Satan's false light, not realizing that he was stilling the glory that belong to Yahweh, and directing it toward himself.

The Greek word **Hupokrites** {Hypocrite} is translated as "**Actor**" in English. Yeshua used this word around 20 times when He was referring to the Pharisees in how they were behaving. He unveiled their wicked intentions and hearts, and for this, they hated Him the more.

Matthew 23:27-28—"*Woe into you, scribes and Pharisees, hypocrites! For you are like unto whited sepulchers, which indeed appear righteous unto men, but within full of dead men's bones, and of all uncleanness. Even so, you also outwardly appear righteous unto men, but within you are full of hypocrisy and iniquity.*" This is the core of those who have the form of godliness.

Q. *__What does, "denying the power thereof," mean__*?
A. The power of Yahweh's word, should be causing the believer to depart from his or her wicked way, to deny themselves, pick up their cross, and to follow after our Lord and savior [**Matthew 16:24**]. The power that is in the Holy Bible should cause that person to love Yahweh more than anything else [**Luke 10:27**], and to love others as yourself [**Matthew 22:39**]. If fact, for the believers, how they are loving other people, is equivalent to how they're loving Yeshua.

It is a frightening thing, for a person who claims to be a student of the bible, but daily, they're not crucifying their fleshly desires [sinful ways], or continues to give in to the same sin or sins, unwilling to forgive those who have hurt them, and can only be religious when they're among other godly people.

False Religion: There are so many false religions and occults in the world today, but why, when there is ONLY one true God, who is Lord of Lords and King of kings? If Adam and Eve would not sinned, then demons couldn't have introduced humans to their false and deceptive light.

Satan, the deceiver, has masterfully crafted numerous false religions, leading humanity astray. These religions, mere human conjectures about God and His desires, are incapable of granting true liberation. Instead, they bind individuals in meaningless rituals and empty traditions. True repentance, it seems, remains elusive within the confines of religious practices, for they focus more on appearance than genuine transformation.

Religion, at its core, asks people to strive for their very best in order to earn favor with God. It places emphasis on personal merit rather than understanding what God truly requires. The notion of righteousness becomes intertwined with good deeds and self-efforts, serving as a means to attain heavenly rewards. However, Christianity stands apart from these man-made religions. Beyond a mere belief system, it offers a profound, life-altering encounter and a vibrant relationship with the one true God.

Rather than being consumed by religious formalities, Christianity urges individuals to experience the grace, mercy, and love of God. It recognizes that true redemption comes not through human works, but through faith in Jesus Christ. It seeks to liberate people from the chains of religiosity and reveals the pathway to genuine freedom and transformation.

Mystery Revealed: The serpent, who was being used by Satan, said to both Adam and Eve, *"God does know that in the day you eat thereof, your eyes shall be open,* **Genesis 4:5**. I want to bring your attention to the word, "***Day or One Thousand Years***," because this is important to know and remember.

But why is this relevant? Because the enemy had but one day or a thousand years is to accomplished his baneful plan against them, once the day or thousand years had expired, the tree of the knowledge of good and evil would have evanesced; never to return again, and they would have had children immediately afterward. This is similar to Satan, when he's bound for a thousand year or, one day in **Revelation 20:1-4**.

When this event took place in the Garden, it was a legitimate thousand years, but in **Revelation 20:1-4**, it will only be for a 24-hour day, not a real thousand years.

How I know this because humans cannot live for a physical thousand years, for it they did, it would break Yahweh's word. Secondly, everyone has to be tempted by the devil, and if he's bound for such a long time, many will have died without being tempted by him, which isn't possible, neither is it fair to those who have been.

But if it's a literal day, then on that day, humans will experience a day unlike any other time, or since the day that sin entered into this world.

The Five Signs of a Religious Spirit:

1. *Deviating from the Word of God*: The first sign of a religious spirit is when you see the person deviating or compromising from the word of God. This spirit causes individuals to inject their own opinions into the Word of God and accept only the Bible scriptures that align with their views. They intentionally ignore verses that challenge their behaviors, hindering any positive change.

2. *Legalism Over Love*: Those with a religious spirit prioritize rules and traditions over compassion and love. They judge others based on strict interpretations of religious laws rather than showing empathy and understanding. If they see a new person enter their church, for instance, a woman wearing a short skirt and tattoos all over her body, they're likely to make her feel very uncomfortable, for they're more concerned about her appearance, rather than her soul getting saved. The love that they have isn't greater than their ability to judge others.

3. *Pride and Self-Righteousness*: Individuals influenced by a religious spirit often display pride and self-righteousness, believing they are superior because of their religious practices and beliefs.

    They are full of hypocrisy, they can see the mote in another person's eyes, but aren't able to view the giant beam in their own; this causes them to focus on other people small faults, but unable to see their big errors.

They hold to grudges. They can intentionally ignore someone and try to avoid their presence, whether in or outside of the church; but during the praise and worship service, can cry out the loudest and pray the longest.

They can even speak in tongues one minute, but to someone who they feel who has hurt or harm them, become silent or speak harshly. They can shout and praise God in the church, while refusing to shake hands with their fellow brothermen.

Religious people believe that their relationship with God is the only thing that matters, and not the relationship between humans, which is also made in the image of Yahweh.

Even when they're wrong, it is almost impossible for them to apologize. They're disrespectful to the true essence of Jesus' nature; love and faith isn't about putting on a show, it's about showing the love that the Holy Spirit has filled one's heart and life with.

And finally, they believe that the anointing upon their life, is more profound than on others. Their church, pastor, choir, and so on, is better than others. Their primary focus is upon people instead of Yahweh. They compare themselves to others, judging other people's relationship with Yahweh instead of focusing upon their own walk with God.

They believe that they're more special than others, that God prefer them over others and therefore, he loves them more.

4. _Lack of Grace and Mercy_: A religious spirit leads to a lack of grace and mercy towards others, as individuals focus more on condemning wrongdoing rather than extending forgiveness and understanding. They are quick to pass harsh judgment upon others for their sins or crimes, but when they're wrong, desiring forgiveness and absolute amnesty.

5. _Resistance to Change: Lastly_, a religious spirit hinders personal growth and transformation by creating resistance to change. Instead of embracing new perspectives and evolving spiritually, those under this spirit cling to rigid beliefs and practices.

They outward appearance is holy, while their inward or heart, has not being transformed. They always focus on outward holiness rather than on inward transformation. What this means is: they can look, sound, and behave holy, but when faced with attacks, whether from demons or humans, their behaviors and response is contradictory to the teachings of the Holy Bible.

They're unaware that holiness starts from the inside, then to the outside; not the other way around. This is one of the things that make religions so deadly, because their holiness stops on the outside, never making its way into their hearts to transform them, causing the love and light of Yahweh to shine greater than the sins or spiritual darkness within this world.

Religion is like a cup that has been cleaned on the outside, but not on the inside and yet, desire for people to drink therefrom, and becomes angry if someone refuses.

CASE THREE: The Misconception of Demons & Possessions

In this chapter, you will learn:

- the ten most common misconceptions about demons
- demon persuasions
- demon possessions

Misconception One: *Satan and Demons does Evil*

This statement is half-truth, because Satan is the essence of evil. For instance, people like: Leopold II of Belgium, Adolf Hitler, Joseh Stalin and so on, were evil people, but Satan doesn't just do evil, but rather, it's source. If Satan no longer existed, all wickedness would no longer exist, and this is why I said, he doesn't just do evil, but rather the source of it.

For instance, many people throughout history could hold the title of being evil or, when they were alive, could be labeled as, 'a very evil person.' And as evil as they were, no one could label them as being the source of evil itself; but Satan can and he is! This means that everyone who has done evil in the past, currently doing wickedness, or will do evil in the future, is due to Satan encouragement.

All wars, famines, robberies, rapes, murderers, greed, divorces, porn, racism, mental abuse, physical abuse, poverty, adultery, fornication, witchcraft, and every other sin would cease to exist, if Satan was removed. Everyone in this world would return back to love, loving and caring for one another. Each person would be full of kindness and generosity, and people would be living longer upon the earth. Everyone would be trying to take care of each other.

Almost every kind of disease and sickness that are currently existing, would be eliminated, because pharmaceutical companies would forsake greed and turn their focus on saving lives, dropping their prices by three-fourths, and every person would have the same health-care that is provided to presidents and other dignitaries. Employers would pay their employees great wages, paying them like if they were a close family member.

In fact, if Satan never existed, we as humans wouldn't even know what death and suffering was, neither would we have experienced it. Instead of visiting a loved one in the cemetery, you and I would be visiting them in the beautiful garden of Eden. We wouldn't have all of these false religions and Yahweh would still be coming down in the cool of the day and fellowshipping with mankind.

Exercise One: Get in a quiet place where you will not be disturbed and relax yourself. Close your eyes and for three minutes, try to imagine you, all of your family, both living and deceased, and as many people as you can possibly think of, living in harmony, while in the garden of Eden. No death, sorrows, sickness, and diseases. ***Stop now and imagine seeing this in your mind for three minutes***.

Imagine seeing and talking with both Adam and Eve. You are even able to talk with the animals within the garden. Every animal there is filled with love and kindness; none of them even knows what violence is, neither can they harm you. You are surrounded by love.

I want you to imagine seeing the tree of life, maybe it's a pure white, like light itself, and the tree of the knowledge of both good and evil, as a beautiful reddish color. They're both sitting in the middle of the garden. ***Stop now and imagine seeing this in your mind for three minutes***.

Now, I want you to imagine hearing God [Yahweh] tell Adam not to eat from the tree of the knowledge of good and evil. But also envision that whenever Yahweh leaves from walking and talking with Adam in the cool of the day [evening time], the serpent immediately go and talks with Eve about disobeying God's commandment to them. But eventually, they succumb to the will of the enemy and is expelled from the garden. ***Stop now and imagine seeing this in your mind for three minutes***.

Now, imagine eight demons ganging up on one of your favorite loved ones, whether alive or dead, just beating them up and you are forced to watch. As your favorite loved one is lying on the ground, bloody and swollen face, one of the demons punches your beloved love one in the face and body again, and as they do, your loved one scream out, and plead for your help, but you aren't able to, due to some kind of force field is prohibiting you.

Whenever the demon punches your loved one, it looks at you with a wicked grin, and says to you, "*what are you going to do about it, you're next?*" And they begin using vulgar language at you. The force-field that is stopping you from reaching, defending, and rescuing your favorite loved one, is the sin in your own life, that you haven't conquered or overcame by the precious blood of the Lamb of Yahweh. ***Stop now and imagine this in your mind for three minutes***.

Inconclusion: Open your eyes, and write a plan on how you're going to deal with and overcome any kind of sin or stronghold in your life, starting today. What bible scriptures you will be using is to combat the sin or sins in your life, in order to save your favorite loved one. Secondly, how you're going to get anything that's demonic out of your home.

Dream Of Mine: In this dream, me and my wife were walking together in a backyard, at a house I used to live in as a child. I turned my head and looked back at my childhood house, but when I did, my wife kept walking. I instructed her to stop and wait for me, but she ignored me and proceeded on. Then she ran into her ex-boyfriend and he immediately begin assaulting her physically.

With all of my heart, I tried to get to them, so I could beat him to death; I was so furious, but something like a forcefield stood within my way, preventing me from saving her. He began kicking and stomping her while on the ground. I was so angry and shouted, No! And said, "I must be dreaming!" And I immediately awaken.

Dream Interpretation:

- Walking together reveals that we were in agreement. The backyard represented that we were both living in our past.

- When I looked back at my childhood house, this meant that I was behaving childish in some areas of our relationship.

- When my wife continues to walk on, even when I called out to her, this meant that she was being rebellious to me and we weren't on the same pace anymore, or in agreement as before.

- When she was being attacked by her ex-boyfriend, this meant that she was going to be attacked by a familiar evil spirit.

- The forcefield represented the sin in my life; you cannot fight a demon, with sin in your life. You must first overcome and get rid of the sin; then will you be able to rescue someone else. The bible says, "They [saints] overcome him [the devil] by the blood of the Lamb, the words of their testimony, for they loved not their lives even unto death," **Revelation 12:11 ESV**. *Special Comment:* Through dreams, Yahweh is able to warn us what's yet to come, so we can escape or go around it. Through certain dreams of mine, I have been able to avoid many pitfalls.

Misconception Two: *Demon's Look Hideous*

Contrary to popular belief, the appearance of demons has been widely misunderstood throughout history, but why? Due to many people failing to study the Bible for themselves and the majority of pastors and teachers are reframing from such a subject, their only depiction of demons are coming from Hollywood.
And most movies have made Satan look reddish, horns, a tail, and sharp teeth, but this description of him is so far from the truth.

The devil's appearance varies across different traditions and religions. Some portray him as a serpent-like creature, some describe him as a handsome man, while some envision him as a powerful looking dragon. In addition, they make demons look like hideous monsters and black shadows that lurks in the night, but this too is wrong and I intend to prove it.

These popular beliefs are strictly contradictory to what the Bible defines their appearance, but are in perfect harmony with what demons want people to think about them, because with such a false belief, they are able to hide behind their good looks and from time to time, reveal themselves and people will think of them as good angels, instead of ugly demons.

Think about the religions in the world today, the ones that their founder proclaimed to have been visited by an angel; now tell me which one of them said or wrote that some disgusting looking angel came to them and revealed Yahweh's message to them? It is always assumed that some good-looking angel, surrounded by a glorious light [2nd **Corinthians 11:14**], came and gave that person some kind of divine revelation from the Creator Himself.

While Yahweh didn't create all of His angels as twins, but rather gave each of them their own look, just like He didn't make every human to look the same in their appearance. He made them beautiful in His own eyes. There were no ugly looking angels. While the Bible doesn't mention the beauty of other angels, it does reveal the immense beauty of Lucifer/Satan in **Ezekiel 28:17**. Just like there is different levels of good-looks in today's world, there were different levels among the angels of Yahweh in heaven.

In conclusion: Demons outward appearances are attractive, but their hearts are very disgusting looking. Therefore, if you see a morally grotesque demon, Yahweh is allowing you to see its heart. If a person encounters an angelic being and it tries to deliver a message to him or her, everything it says, should be examine by what is already written in the Holy Bible, and if the angel contradicts anything that is written, the person should immediately rebuke that angel in Yeshua's name: commanding it to leave in Jesus' name.

Misconception Three: *About Demon Possession:*

When we read about demon possessions in the Bible, we see people behaving irrationally, doing such things as foaming at the mouth, cutting themselves, possessing supernatural strength, screaming or crying out loud, living in a cemetery, and attempting suicide, but not all people were mimicking these traits [**Mark 5:1-5 & 9:21-22**] who were possessed by demons.

For instance, Mary, called Magdalene, was possessed with seven demons [**Luke 8:2**] and yet, she didn't do any of the behaviors I just described. I am writing about demon possession, because it is still real and happening in today's world, and now I will reveal it. My point is, a person can be demon possessed without foaming at the mouth, cutting themselves, and attempting to commit suicide.

A person is demon possessed when he or she loses their control to stop doing wicked or evil behaviors and actions. Even when they try to stop, they're unable to do so. There are different levels of possessions. The more demons they have within, the greater they're going to behave unseemly.

There are some demons that are stronger than other ones, or wickeder. **Matthew 12:43-45**. *"When an unclean spirit goes out of a man, he goes through dry places, seeking rest, and finds none. Then he says, 'I will return to my house from which I came.' And when he comes, he finds it empty, swept, and put in order. Then he goes and takes with him seven **other spirits more wicked than himself**, and they enter and dwell there; and the last state of that man is worse than the first. So shall it also be with this wicked generation."*

Q. But what makes some demons wickeder than other ones?
A. While ever demons govern over a particular sin, a few rules over more, causing them to be more wicked and able to possess a stronger hold on their victims. Think of them as venomous snakes, while all of them have poison and are able to kill an animal or another person, some have toxin that could kill up to 100 individuals, and an animal as big as an elephant.

<u>Allow me to rewrite Matthew 12:43-45, in order to bring better clarity</u>. When a demon is cast out of a person [because it will not leave on its own], it will go and dwell among people who are susceptible and more likely to receive it. But if the people its among will not accept the unclean spirit, it will return back to its original host. And when it discovers that this individual hasn't returned to evil, but the person hasn't been filled with the Holy Spirit, it will not immediately try to reenter into him or her again, but will go and find seven other demons, like its self, but stronger in wickedness.

Then all eight of them will go and enter into that individual who hasn't been filled with the Holy Spirit. Now, the person is worse than before, because the additional seven evil spirits are bringing in new sinful things into the person's mind and life. Therefore, so shall it be like this current generation.

<u>Special Information</u>: Whenever a person gets delivered from an evil spirit, it is dangerous for him or her to not be filled with the Holy Spirit and secondly, they should not return to any of their previous sins, except that

demon will go and gather seven additional evil spirits and reenter that person, making things much worse for them.

Misconception Four: *All Demons Are The Same*

While all demons are evil, not all of them mimic the same characteristics. For instance, while some of them promote sexual perversion, another one will try to convince a person to be a serial killer or to engage in debauchery, and so on.

What are demons trying to pull you into? Remember, it's important for you to stop a bad behavior now, so your children don't become overcome by it. Demons are trying to pull the individual into their previous sins.

Exercise: Write down on a sheet of paper, what you believe is a stronghold for you, and how you plan on using bible scriptures to stop it. A stronghold is any kind of sinful thing that's you haven't overcome yet.

Misconception Five: *Demons and the Fallen Angels are different*

With a growing number of religious people are believing that demons and the fallen angels are different beings, it is important that we return to the bible in order to know the real truth, rather than relying upon our own intellect. In the bible, the names that are related to evil spirit is:

- Lucifer/Hêlēl
- Beelzebub
- Belial
- Abandon/Apollyon

Titles that are giving to them or to the devil himself are:

- The Old Serpent
- Satan
- Devil
- The Dragon
- The Accuser
- Unclean Spirits
- Familiar Spirits
- The Temper
- The Wicked One
- The Evil One
- The Enemy
- The Thief
- The Liar
- The Father of Lies
- Murderer
- Ruler of this World
- Deceiver
- God of this World
- Angel of Light
- Adversary
- Roaring Lion
- Angel of the Abyss
- Evil Spirit(s)
- Lying Spirit
- Prince of this World
- Prince of Demons

While there is no mention of the word "demon" in the bible, it is widely accepted that the words "devils and demons" are interchangeable.

Misconception Six: ***Satanist People Can Control Demons***

Many people believe that satanist and those who practice any form of witchcraft, are able to control demons. I knew of a woman who was a high priestess witch and others who practice sorcery; and in the beginning, demons did permit those persons to control them, but as they begin to grow in the dark arts, those same demons took back their powers, and enslaved the same individual. You see, that was a part of their deception, to allow the person to gain temporary control over them, until he or she sought more power and authority over them, and then the demons would reverse the role, become master over that human.

And once the demons become their masters, he or she is forced to release their will and kingdom upon the earth, are face punishment.

When that high priestess witch, tried to abandon that practice, she said that demons would visit her house in the night, slamming doors and darken shadows running throughout her home. The demons told her, that she was forbidding to leave, or else, they would kill her.
Eventually, she moved to another city, and she said the same thing happen in her new home; doors slamming, her bed begin to levitate, and hearing strange things. About a month later, her witch sister and brethren found her and commanded her to return to the order, or else face the consequences. She told them that she wanted to become a Christian and they laugh at her and told her that satanists have more power than Christians.

Then something unique happened, she mentioned the blood of Jesus, and when she did, they shook and looked very worried and said, "Don't never mention about that again!"

Then the woman spoke about the blood of Jesus again, and they literally ran out of her house and never came back.
Then she had a pastor to come and anoint her house, and immediately, the demons left her home and never bothered her again.

Misconception Seven: ***Demons Just Want People To Do Evil***

While it is true that demons desire for everyone to do evil, this isn't their main objective, because if a person does wrong, he or she can also repent of their sin or sins, and turn to Yeshua. So, then, what do all demons really want from everyone? They're desiring for someone who is willing and able to release their kingdom upon the earth.

I will reveal a mystery to you: Yeshua said, "*The kingdom of God is within you,* "**Luke 17:21**." Satan tries to copy the things of Yahweh and therefore, he desires for his kingdom of darkness to dwell in every human. Once this kingdom of darkness is released in that person life, then they will be able to release it into the lives of others, causing their followers and anyone that is connected to them, to abide and the same false light they're walking in, and finally, it can be unleashed into the world.

Misception Eight: *Satan Can't Tell The Truth*

Many Christians believe that the devil is unable to tell the truth, and perhaps this belief came about due to Jesus saying, "*He [the devil] is a liar, and doesn't abide in the truth, because there isn't any in him,*" **John 8:45**. While Yeshua reveals that Satan is a liar, He wasn't saying that the devil isn't capable of telling someone the truth, but rather he will not continue telling it.

Satan, when trying to tempt Jesus to do wrong, said to Him, "He {Yahweh} will give His angels charge over you, if you dash your foot against the stone; he was telling the truth, because this was written in **Psalm 91:11-12**, but whenever Satan reveal the truth about something, it will be a verse to get the individual to commit sin, to break Yahweh's commandment, and or to convince that individual to view God negatively.

Satan will try to convince a believer that if they sin, it's okay, and if they do it again, it's okay and will not suffer any of the consequences for it, because they are under grace [**Romans 6:15**], not under the law, but the grace that we have obtained through Jesus Christ, in no way gives the believer a free pass to do whatsoever they desire, without any kind of repercussions.

"*What then? Shall we sin because we are not under the law, but under grace? By no means! Do you not know that if you present yourselves to anyone as obedient slaves, you are slaves of the one whom you obey, either of sin, which leads to death, or of obedience, which leads to righteousness? But thanks be to God that you who were once slaves of sin have become obedient from the heart to the standard of teaching to which you were committed. And having been set free from sin, have become slaves of righteousness.*" **Romans 6:15-18 ESV**.

Brothers and sisters in Christ Jesus, be not deceived, grace doesn't give us a free ticket or license to sin, but rather enable us to live a sin-free life.

Misconception Nine: *Demons Are Against Each Other*

Some people actually believe that demons war against one another, but this is totally false. While they hate each other, they work in cohesion and all share a common goal, to destroy as many souls as possible.
Yeshua said, *"Every kingdom divided against itself is brought to desolation; and every city or house divided against itself shall not stand. And if Satan cast out Satan, he is divided against himself, how then will his kingdom stand?"* **Matthew 12:25-26**. This bible verse absolutely proves that demons are working in cahoots. Unlike humans, who fight against among themselves, over feeble reasons.

Something to think about: I have never, in all of my days, seen witches and warlocks fight among themselves like religious people do. I have witness pastors, more interested in belittling and or fighting against the ministries of other church leaders, rather than obeying Yeshua, and to compel sinners to come and be saved [**Luke 14:23**].

It's a common thing to see other pastors and teachers, projecting the image or confessing that the anointing upon their lives, are greater than others, because they paid or worked hard for it, which is both asinine and preposterous. The last time I checked, my bible informs me that Christ was the one who suffered and died for us, and therefore, it is His anointing, not theirs!

There's only one who anoints for a particular office within the fivefold ministry, but we all may have different gifts. For instance, if Yeshua anoints a man to pastor, and anoints a woman to evangelize, the anointing that is upon the pastor's life, wouldn't be stronger than the one on the evangelist's life.

The anointing on Elisha's life, wasn't stronger than his teacher, Elijah. Just because Elisha preformed more miracles, doesn't imply that the anointing on his life was more profound. Some people are confusing the anointing with the gifts. The anointing covers the gifts within the person's life, and therefore, cannot become stronger nor lesser.

To say one person's anointing is stronger than another, makes as much sense as hearing someone say, my sail boat is better and stronger than yours, because while yours were able to withstand the waves of the

Atlantic Ocean, mine was able to survive the waves of the Pacific Ocean, in which you know is deeper than the Atlantic.

Yahweh doesn't anoint someone with a stronger or lesser anointing, because He is the empowerment behind the anointing itself, and therefore, He cannot increase or decrease!

Misconception 10: *Demons Can Read A Person's Mind*

Demons, while they're spirits, are not able to read people's minds; but what they try to do is to influence the person to be in a high-risk situation, a place where they're likely to commit a sinful act, and then put a corrupt thought within their mind at that very moment. Only Yahweh is able to read a person's mind and know what that individual is going to do, before they actually do it.

Understanding Demon Persuasions and Possessions Demons:

Demon Persuasions:

"But every man [person] is tempted, when he [or she] is drawn away by their own lust, and enticed. Then when lust has conceived, it brings forth sin: and sin, when it is finished [with that person], brings forth death," **James 1:14-15**.

Before a person can become demon possessed, they will undergo two more steps, which is *persuasion* and *cogent stages*.

Persuasion Stage:

Demon persuasion is the method devils uses to entrap, enslave, and finally, to possess an individual. The persuasion begins when the person begins hearing an inner voice, trying to entice them to do something that's immoral, impractical, or unethical. Something within their mind is making a strong case for them to engage in wrong environments, thoughts, feelings, behaviors, and or activities. Demons cannot possess a child of God, but a Christian can be under demon's persuasions, and that's why we must beware of their tricks and walk daily within the Holy Spirit [**Galatians 5:16-21**].

Before demons can possess someone, they must successfully persuade the person to yield to his or her own weaknesses or sinful nature. After doing that particular sin for 21 days or longer, if the person attempts to stop, the urge to avoid that sin becomes very difficult. The final stage is when the person gives those demons complete access into their mind, then it becomes a possession.

But, in this section, I will elucidate more on the persuasion. Think of the persuasion as a seed, that demons are trying to plant within that person's mind. And once the person gives in to that sin, the seed is not only planted within the soil of their mind, but their behavior and action behave like water and sunlight to that seed, giving it the nutrients needed to take root and to grow properly. Shortly after yielding to their sinful desire, the person may notice that they're no longer tempted to do that sin within that hour again, and may actually pray and ask for forgiveness if they're religious. But within a few hours later, or maybe the next day, he or she is likely to repeat that same sin again.

But why isn't the person tempted to immediately repeat the sin again, when they have done it? This is because the demon or demons, temporary left the person's environment, in order to gather more reinforcements or additional demons, is to help them attempt and to obtain a greater stronghold over that person's life. They don't want to take any kind of chance, that the person might actually repent, turning away from their sin. Ergo, with the additional demons, they believe it will greatly increase their odds, that that person will repeat the sin again and again, and so on.

The Irresistible Urges:
After the persuasions stage, the next form of attack is what I call: "*The Irresistible Urges*." Once at this point, quitting the sinful act becomes almost impossible. The demons will not stop annoying or reminding that individual to do wrong, he or she may experience nervousness, anxiety, depression, anger, and unable to release positive endorphins, until they yield to it, and like before, the demons will recede, but only temporary, until they bring back more demons is to tempt that person.

At this stage, whenever the person repeats the sin, not all of the demons will leave their environment as before, but the stronger ones will remain with that individual, while the weaker ones will go and draw in additional ones, bringing them to that person, for hopes of an invasion.

Important Intel: If the person attended church regularly, and made it to this stage, he or she is likely to quit attending and a significant negative change will be noticed within them. This is because more of the demon's personalities will begin to manifest itself through the person's behavior and actions. For example, in the past, he or she might have talked about godly things and were excited to do so, but at the irresistible stage, you will notice that they're uncomfortable discussing godly topics and subject to isolate themselves from other saints. It is a common thing to see them connecting with people who are being attacked by the similar demons as they are.

Demon Possession:

But first, let's understand exactly what is a possession. Basically, a possession implies that someone has control over a thing, person, or an object. It is considered to be their property or the rights to something. While all demon possessions are serious and should be taken as such, I will be revealing two kinds of possessions. For instance, the man who had a legion of demons, I will refer to as "***possession without control***, while when the person has fewer demons in them, like Mary of Magdalena, I will be referring to as "***possession with some control***."

Signs of a person Possessed Without Control   (The Man with Legion)

- When they try to stop doing something wrong, the negative urges override their will-power
- They are unable to control their destructive words, they say things to love ones and friends that are highly offensive, and while they will apologize, shortly afterwards, they're saying something else that is extremely hurtful
- Suicidal tendencies   • Chanting   • Foaming the mouth whenever a Christian is nearby
- At times or oftentimes, trying to harm oneself or, something else
- Their thoughts, imagination, and core beliefs continual to focus on wickedness
- Oftentimes, crying or yelling out for no good reason

Signs of a person Possessed With Limited Control   (Mary Magdalena)

- They can only stop doing something wrong for a short period of time, maybe a month or two and then, return back doing it. This is because the urges from the demons, overrides the person's desire to stop doing it.
- They might ask God for forgiveness, but they're unable to truly repent

- Unable to stop the pernicious inner voices in the head. Sometimes, they feel like a person who is suffering from schizophrenia

Q. How does a person get or become possessed by demons?
A. Before revealing the things that can open up a person for demon possessions, let me make it perfectly clear that *NO true Christian can be demon possessed*! *But they can be oppressed*!
These lists of things are the quickest ways to become demon possessed:
- People who practice dark magic, whether white or black
- psychics
- mediums
- gurus
- spiritists
- warlocks
- witches
- sorcery
- wizard
- necromancer
- charmer
- divination
- soothsayer
- augur
- Yoga
- occult practices
- Wicca
- clairvoyance
- ancestor worship
- Voodoo
- become a satanist
- trying to cast demons out of a person who's possessed, without having the Holy Spirit
- Spirit Guides

Additional Ways:
- Playing with a Ouija Board
- Tarot Cards
- Palm Readings
- Crystal Balls
- Seeking help from a gypsy and fortune telling
- Some forms of mediation
- Reading Horoscopes

Current Plans for Demon Possession:

While the list above unveils the quickest ways to become demon possessed, lets discuss how they have changed some of their strategies, in order to possess people in the 21st century.

Possession One: *Through Certain Music, Songs, and Dances*

The Music: Music has a profound impact on our emotions and well-being. Music has the ability to stir up memories that we had forgotten about. It can also greatly impact our mood and overall mental state. Music can be very therapeutic, bring healing to our wounded heart, as well as causing aggression. It can also affect how the person reacts to certain situations and how they're communicating with others. Music is known as a universal language that transcends barriers and unites individuals from different cultures and backgrounds. It can bring people together, creating stronger bonds, or it can tear them apart, creating discord among once close allies. In conclusion, music is far more than just sounds. It possesses the ability to change a person's life.

Please keep in mind that Lucifer, before his fall, was over the music and therefore, knows the effects it can have over people's impressionable minds in today's world. Just as the Father, Son, and Holy Spirit is one [**1st John 5:7**], and the spirit, water, and blood is one [**1st John 5:8**], so is music, singing, and dancing. This is why all three can be seen at concerts, parties, on television, etc. Satan know that when this trio comes together, it will either draw holy angels or unclean spirits to the person who are preforming such things.

<u>*Songs*</u>: Remember, songs are words put together with harmony; and the bible says that both death and life are in our words [**Proverbs 18:21**]. Therefore, whenever you're listening to someone sing, from the words being said within the song, is either feeding the listener soul with death or life, and demons know this.

Whenever a person is listening to songs that is full of death, they are drawing certain devils to their current location and enabling them to perform whatsoever words being said within it. For instance, if a man oftentimes listens to lyrics in a song that are misogynistic, then when those evil spirits are drawn to him, they will farther indoctrinate his mind with hatred, causing him to think and to reminisce with his buddies just how terrible women are. He will teach other young men how to become distrustful of all women and to view them as devils.
Every woman who has hurt him, will be on full display, during his conversation with whosoever talks with him.

Or if a young lady listens to songs that glorifies being whorish. As she's listens and sing along, and maybe dance to that terrible song, devils will invade her territory and impregnate her susceptible mind with whorish ideals, causing her to dance seductively, wearing alluring clothing, and to speak like a woman who has little to no standards, morals, and values. The devils will cause her to sell her body to the highest bidder, like at an auction.

<u>*Special Comment*</u>: Many people have played certain song backwards, and when they did, the singer was giving Satan praise or glory.

<u>**Dances**</u>: Dancing is a very powerful form of self-expression, and is linked to praise and worship. Dancing also has a profound impact on our mental state. It releases endorphins, those feel-good hormones that boost our mood and reduce stress levels. Therefore, demons become extremely stimulated at certain dances, especially the seductive ones. Less than one minute after

a person begins performing sexual dances, demons surround that individual and becomes elated, and put within their soul the ideal to commit fornication or, adultery.

In conclusion: The more a person submits to sinful urges, their ability to resist negative temptations becomes almost impossible. And if they're not covered by the precious blood of Jesus Christ, through these songs, musical instruments, and dances, demons will eventually enter into that person, and if enough of them enter that individual, he or she will become possessed.

So, then in the story where the man was possessed with legions [**Mark 5:1-5**], a legion ranged from 3 to 6 thousand soldiers, in this case, demons, were abiding within this man. Remember what I said, demons, while all are evil, they don't all share the same behaviors, and with different demons, you have different attitudes and agendas. No offense, but think of a person who's suffering from extreme bipolar or from Dissociate Identity Disorder [DID], while most people view these as medical disorders, they are actually demons who are attempting and, in some situations, controlling that person's behaviors; *this isn't to say that people with these disorders are demon possessed.*

Possession Two: *Demons Working Through Certain Movies, Television Programs & social media*

In times past, demons needed for a person to read some spell book and repeat certain words while sitting in the middle of a pentagram and candles, in order to possess the individual. But nowadays, all they need is a person to either go to the movies or, just sit before their television or computer, and can achieve the same results. You see, most movies and television programs will all have some form of witchcraft within it. And as the viewer is watching these kinds of movies, demons are entering the home and, attempting to bewitch that individual, as to possess him or her.

Special Comment: In the time of writing the manuscript for these movies, oftentimes, the producers will have some real witches, as to give their input on what words, symbols, and sounds needs to be within the movie, in order to release demons into their viewers homes. While I cannot list all of the movies that contain witchcraft, because it would be too much; here's a list of the most well-known:

Drama   **Action**

1. The Craft
2. Bewitched
3. Practical Magic
4. Harry Potter Trilogy
5. The Love Witch
6. Into the Woods
7. Suspiria
8. Beautiful Creatures
9. The House with a clock In its walls
10. Hocus Pocus
11. Eve's Bayou
12. Mirror Mirror
13. Teen Witch
14. Hansel & Gretel: Witch Hunter
15. Spirited Away
16. The Wizard of Oz
17. Matilda
18. An American Haunting
19. Maleficent
20. Twitches

1. Scooby-Doo & the witch's ghost
2. Lord of the Rings trilogy
3. Doctor Strange Trilogy
4. The Avenger's Trilogy
5. Ahsoka Tano Series
6. Dungeons & Dragons Series
7. Buffy the Vampire Slayer
8. The Little Mermaid
9. Good Omens
10. The Green Knight
11. Stardust
12. Fantastic Beasts & where to find them series
13. Wanda Vision
14. The Conjuring
15. Antichrist (2009) movie
16. Merlin Series
17. Excalibur
18. Xena: Warrior Princess
19. Sleepy Hollow

Hellboy

Watching movies like these and such like, are doorways for demons to enter a person's home, and afterwards, into their body and lives. Remember, before they can live in a person's body, they must first gain access into their mind, then they can possess that individual.

Just think about all of the asinine things that are seen on social media, and the folks who are watching and supporting them. People are doing disgusting and demonic things, in order to convince others to follow them. Here me, these clowns are not coming up with these offensive ideals on their own, no, but rather its demons instructing them on what to do, in order to persuade viewers to follow them. Because, as these people are following those disturbed individuals, they're also following after demons.

Possession Three: *Through Certain Video Games*

Video Games: There has been a longstanding debate about whether certain video games can act as a conduit for Satan's influence, particularly those that contain explicit content such as sex, violence, vulgar language, theft,

and more. These things serve as a breeding ground for darkness and vice. Exposure to such explicit content can desensitize individuals, eroding their moral compass and encouraging unethical behavior.
Satan can exploit these games by subtly manipulating players' minds, blurring the lines between virtual and real-world actions. The immersive nature of certain video games can make it easier for malicious thoughts and intentions to take root, ultimately paving the way for satanic influence.

With their mature themes and explicit content, they desensitize players to immoral behavior. The
constant exposure to virtual violence, offensive language, and themes of theft can shape the moral compass of individuals, leading them down a dangerous path.

Satan potentially exploit these games as a tool to gradually erode the values upheld in society. By normalizing behaviors condemned by traditional beliefs, the games may subtly encourage players to engage in real-life actions that go against moral principles.

True Story: But I remember one day, when I was writing another book on demons, and in a moment time, I became very sleepy. The night before, I had gotten plenty of sleep and I wasn't tired. So, then I got up and started to play one of my video games, and instantly I woke up. I immediately stop playing and rebuke the enemy in Jesus' name. Because I realized that it was a trick of Satan. He didn't want me to expose him and his demons, so he attacked me with sleep. In Jesus' name did I rebuked him and the feeling of sleep immediately left me and I was able to continue my work for my Lord God.

The video games I have are the older ones, when games weren't as filthy as the latest ones. Nowadays, most video games contain sex, witchcraft, theft, drugs, murder, and so on. There are people who are actually getting paid for playing games, [online gamers]. I have seen people play violent games for hours, only taking breaks to use the bathroom and to eat, and then immediately resume playing, but cannot spend 30 minutes studying their bible and praying. Demons love whenever people use their limited and yet precious time, doing things that glorify either themselves, or other people.

Visiting An Older Sister: One day, I was visiting my third oldest sister, and during that time, I felt asleep. But when I awaken, her youngest son was playing a video game, in which I could feel the presence of demon spirits. I immediately inform him of what I was feeling and told his mother. When she entered the basement in where he was playing, she immediately insisted that he stop and to remove that game from their home. Demons can attach themselves to certain objects as well, like video and board games.

Social Media: It is often said that Satan works in mysterious ways, and in the age of technology, social media has become one of his unholy playgrounds. Through the screens that now dominate our lives, the dark forces of manipulation and deception thrive, wreaking havoc on the minds and souls of unsuspecting individuals.

Hidden beneath the facade of connectivity and entertainment, satanic influences can be found destroying people's minds with repulsive scenes that penetrate the depths of human depravity. These images and videos, like grotesque fantasies, lure the weak-willed into a twisted obsession.

Satan's corruptive power manifests itself in the most despicable of acts, such as the portrayal of individuals eating out of toilets or engaging in seductive dances that degrade the sanctity of human intimacy. He revels in promoting violence, fueling online fights that spill over into the real world, engendering chaos and destruction.

Through social media, Satan entices humanity towards darker desires, exploiting our vulnerabilities and leading us astray. We must remain vigilant and shield ourselves from these sinister influences, for in the virtual realm, the battle for our souls' rages on.

CASE FOUR: <u>The Great Deceiver</u>

After studying this chapter, you should be able to:
- know the difference between lies versus deception
- the different kind of lies
- what kind of liar is Satan

Let's read what Jesus/Yeshua said to the children of the devil, about their father, Satan: *"Why is my language not clear to you? Because you are unable to hear what I say. You belong to your father, the devil, and you want to carry out your father's desires. He was a murderer from the beginning, not holding to the truth, for there is no truth in him. When he lies, he speaks his native language, for he is a liar and the father of lies,"* **John 8:43-44 NIV**. Sometimes, when reading these words, a person can miss just how serious they are, that Yeshua was conveying to us about Satan; so, then allow me to elucidate.

Father And Inventor Of Lies:

Satan isn't just a master liar and deceiver, he's, their father. If you're a good parent, you know how you would protect your children, and how protective are you over them; well, Satan feels the same way about his beloved lies and deceptions, because they're his children. If you took away his lies and deceptions, they he and his demons would cease to exist anymore.

Special Comment: The only thing that Satan loves more than himself, is the lies he tells to himself, his fallen angels, and to humans. Satan loves his lies so much, and becomes extremely offended when a human doesn't receive it. It would be as if someone refuses to accept one of your beloved children, as if they were too good. Ergo, Satan feel very hurt whenever someone repudiates one of his lies which came from his nocuous heart.

Yeshua told the people why they couldn't understand what He was telling them, because they were of their spiritual father, the devil, and the desire of him will they do. The lies from the devil, prohibit them from hearing and understanding Yeshua.

Next, He told them that they were carrying out their father's will. Yeshua defines Satan as both a murderer and liar, since the beginning. His lies didn't begin in the book of Genesis, but rather in eternity, when he beguiled one-third of the host of Yahweh. So, then before time existed as we know it, he had already sinned against Yahweh.

Whenever Satan and his demons tell people lies, they're literally describing their personalities to them. Please, don't forget, demons know how to speak the truth, they just won't continue speaking it. But if they do speak the truth, it will be to get the person to commit sin or to do wrong.

Special Comment: Demons aren't able to have full fellowship and effective communication, until they can convince the person to become fluent in their language, which is based on lies and deceptions.
I want to reveal to those who aren't familiar with the many different kinds of lies and deceptions of the devil, so whenever you decide to read the bible again, you will know just how deadly and sadistic, he and his unclean spirits are.

Liars and deceivers are often used interchangeably, but there is indeed a subtle distinction between the two. While both engage in dishonesty, their motives and methods differ significantly.

A liar is someone who intentionally communicates false information with the explicit intention of misleading others. They fabricate stories or misrepresent facts, typically to benefit themselves or avoid negative consequences. The lies they tell are often deliberate and calculated.

On the other hand, a deceiver is someone who manipulates the truth by withholding information, distorting facts, or using strategic trickery to create a false perception or impression. Deceivers are skilled in presenting a twisted version of reality while leaving out crucial details, exploiting loopholes in communication.

In essence, the main difference lies in the intent and approach. A liar is overtly dishonest and fulfills their agenda through outright fabrication, while a deceiver masks the truth through manipulation and selective disclosure. Both have the potential to damage trust and cause harm, but understanding the nuances helps in identifying their tactics and protecting ourselves from their snares.

What are the differences between lies versus deception?

Lying

1. Can be done to protect or harm someone
2. To make a deliberate false statement
3. Can cause people to fight one another
4. Can enslave families
5. Can cause people to believe false religion
6. Can cause a person's heart to become
Bitter and affect their children
7. Lies causes the heart to become harden
8. Lies told with emphasis will direct the
People's focus

Deception

1. Is mostly done with intentions to harm someone
2. Causing others to believe something that isn't true
3. Can cause nations to war against one another

4. Can enslave generations
5. Can create false religions
6. Can cause a nation to become hateful and racist
7. Deception causes a nation of people to grieve
8. Deception told with assertiveness will mislead the world

<u>**White Lies:**</u> What is a white lie? A white lie is a seemingly harmless falsehood told to avoid confrontation, spare someone's feelings, or simply create a more comfortable environment. While they may appear innocent, white lies can have harmful effects on both the person who tells them and the person being deceived.

One of the negative consequences of white lies is the erosion of trust. When we repeatedly resort to deception, even for the noblest reasons, people start questioning our honesty and integrity. Additionally, white lies can prevent individuals from facing realities and making informed decisions. By concealing the truth, we rob others of the opportunity to learn and grow.

Moreover, white lies often create a vicious cycle. Once we start down the path of deception, it becomes easier to continue lying, potentially leading to more significant falsehoods. Furthermore, the guilt and anxiety that accompany the perpetuation of white lies can take a toll on our mental and emotional well-being.

While it may be tempting to resort to white lies to avoid discomfort, it is important to recognize their potential harmful effects. Building trust through open communication and facing difficult truths is ultimately more beneficial for all parties involved.

Q. How demons are actively working through white lies?
A. While the vast majority of people downplays the significance of white lies, viewing them as a lesser danger than the other ones, but they are gateways into the others. To de-emphasize white lies, is equivalent to saying and believing that white magic is okay, because the person isn't practicing black magic.

Demons are master manipulators, harnessing the power of white lies to deceive and lead people astray. These sinister creatures have perfected the art of trickery, using falsehoods to disguised as harmless truths to exploit vulnerabilities in human nature.

Their web of deceit is intricately woven, strategically crafted to misguide anyone who isn't walking daily in the Holy Spirit. The demons capitalize on the inherent trust we place in seemingly innocent white lies, exploiting our desire for validation, acceptance, and understanding.
Their methods are insidious, often camouflaging their true intentions behind half-truths and carefully constructed narratives.

Oftentimes, demons use white lies to beguile Christians who only read the bible, but not studying as they are instructed to do [**2ⁿᵈ Timothy 2:15**]. And because they're not studying, demons are able to distort their understanding while reading or hearing the word of Yahweh.

Again, through demon's white lies, they have convinced some believers to make end-times movies, showing how a few Christians who missed the rapture, will moderately suffer under the antichrist and false prophet new regime, who Satan himself will give the kingdoms of the world to the beast, will be capable to damage irreparably their reputation, by exposing their malicious schemes, and to bring about the antichrist and false prophet's demise. Now, how absurd and asinine does that sound!

Yeshua clearly tells us [**Matthew 25:1-13**], that there were ten virgins, five were wise and five foolish. The wise took oil in their lamps, but the foolish didn't. While all of them were sleeping, there was a cry heard, telling them that the bridegroom was coming.

The foolish ones [*the ones who had run out of oil*] asked to borrow from those who had enough, but the wise denied their request, but instructed them to buy from those who sold it. When the foolish went back to purchased more, the bridegroom came and only took those who were ready, and when the foolish returned and requested access in, it was denied.

The virgins represent the church or believers. The light and oil represent our relationship with Yeshua: *"You are the light of this world. A city that is set on a hill cannot be hid. Neither do men light a candle, and put it under a bushel, but on a candlestick; and it gives light unto all that are in the house. Let your light so shine before men, that they may see your good works, and glorify your Father which is in heaven,"* **Matthew 5:14-16**.

<u>Inconclusion</u>: The foolish virgins, didn't let their light [*the light of Jesus*] shine in this wicked world, but rather hid it [*not taking a stand for Jesus Christ and doing the work they were called to do*]. A person's walk with

Yahweh, should and must bring glory to God the Holy Father, and to Him alone. So, then the foolish brought glory to themselves, rather than to Yahweh.

It is only through studying the word of Yahweh, seeking His face, accepting Yeshua as the Son of Yahweh, and doing what He has called the person to do in this world, can they discern and break free from the clutches of these deceitful beings, reclaiming our path and forging a future guided by truth and authenticity.

Exercise: On a separate sheet of paper, write how you feel about white lies, and should you use them in certain cases. Next, whenever tells you a white lie, how does it make you feel and why.

Rhetorical Questions: A rhetorical question is a figure of speech that is posed for effect rather than seeking an actual answer. It is commonly used to make a point or to emphasize a particular idea. Now, let's explore how Satan can effectively set someone up using a rhetorical question.

The devil can use a rhetorical question strategically to subtly manipulate someone's perception or provoke thought. By carefully crafting a question that implies a certain answer or presumes a specific viewpoint, he can guide the conversation towards his desired outcome.

For instance, the serpent asked Eve, "*Did Yahweh really say?*" This question planted a seed of suspicion, raising eyebrows and prompted her to ponder if God really meant what she thought He said.

By framing the question in a way that captured Eve's attention and appeals to her emotions or beliefs, the serpent could subtly influence her thoughts or actions without overtly stating her intentions. It is essential to remember that rhetorical questions should be used ethically, respecting the boundaries of honesty and fairness while still getting the desired message across.

Lies of Omission: The lie of omission refers to the act of deliberately withholding or leaving out important information or details, resulting in a distorted or incomplete version of the truth. Unlike a direct lie, where one actively fabricates false information, a lie of omission occurs when someone purposefully chooses not to disclose facts or relevant information.

The danger of the lies of omission, exist in the potential to deceive or mislead others. By deliberately withholding crucial information, individuals can manipulate the perception of truth and control the narrative in their favor. This act of deceit can have serious consequences, both in personal relationships and larger societal contexts.

Example of the lie of omission in action: A father offer to buy his college son a car, if he does his best. So, he asks his son, "how are you doing in school?" His son replies, "Dad, I am working very hard but I'm still having some trouble. I am averaging a "C" level grade." But he intentional neglected to mention that he's hanging out with friends and going to parties instead of studying like he should be. So, then based on the assumption that his son is doing his very best, he buys him a vehicle.

In personal relationships, lies of omission can erode trust and destroy the foundation of honesty. When people rely on each other for transparent communication, the deliberate absence of important facts can lead to misunderstandings, conflicts, and even the collapse of relationships.

On a larger scale, lies of omission can have significant societal implications, as they can influence public opinion, skew political discourse, or distort crucial decision-making processes. In journalism, for instance, the omission of key facts can change the entire context of a story, leading to biased reporting and manipulation of public perception.

Ultimately, lies of omission undermine the principles of integrity, transparency, and trust, therefore warranting caution and vigilance in both personal and communal spheres.

The serpent used the lie of omission on Eve when it said, "*You shall not surly die,*" **Genesis 4:4**. The enemy knew that it wasn't just about a physical death, but rather a spiritual one. That by disobeying Yahweh, their lives would never be the same. You see, demons knew what it felt like to be disconnected from Yahweh, because they themselves had experienced firsthand, and they wanted Adam and Eve to share their dread.

Exercise: How often do you leave out information, whether its significate or small, when talking with someone? How often do you omit intel when talking with someone?

Lies of Commission: The lie of commission refers to a deliberate act of spreading false information or distorting the truth. When someone engages in a lie of commission, they actively fabricate facts or intentionally deceive others. This form of lying can have significant consequences and dangers.

One of the major dangers of the lie of commission is the erosion of trust. When individuals consistently engage in spreading falsehoods, it erodes the trust others have in them and in the information they provide. This can lead to polarization and division within communities and society as a whole. And once truth is damaged, the relationship suffers and possible, it will come to an end.

Another danger of lies of commission is the potential for harm. False information can have real-world consequences, causing panic, confusion, or even physical harm. In today's digital age, where information spreads rapidly, the damage caused by lies of commission can escalate quickly.

Something to think about: Wars and lies have been intertwined throughout history, their connection undeniably powerful. It is a troubling truth that many conflicts around the world have been instigated and fueled by the dissemination of falsehoods. Lies breed suspicion, fabricate fear, and manipulate perceptions, creating a perfect breeding ground for hostilities to take root.

In the realm of wars, lies often serve as a catalyst, perpetuating a cycle of mistrust and vengeance. Governments and leaders have repeatedly resorted to distorting facts, manipulating narratives, and spreading propaganda to rally support for their agendas or demonize their adversaries. These deliberate deceptions distort reality and justify the unthinkable, as societies and individuals become pawns in the game of geopolitical power struggles.

However, it is crucial to acknowledge that not all conflicts are solely fueled by lies. Complex factors like resource disputes, ideological differences, and historical grievances also contribute to the outbreak of wars. Nevertheless, it is undeniable that lies play a significant role in exacerbating tensions and escalating conflicts. To prevent future wars, it is essential to confront the lies that permeate our world, seek truth and transparency, and strive for open and honest dialogue. Only then can we hope to break free from the destructive cycle of wars driven by lies.

Furthermore, lies of commission can have long-lasting effects on relationships and reputations. Once trust is broken, it is not easily regained. People may question the credibility and integrity of those who have engaged in deliberate deception, tarnishing their reputation and potentially hindering future opportunities.

In conclusion, the lie of commission is the deliberate act of spreading false information, which poses dangers such as the erosion of trust, potential harm, and damage to one's reputation. It is essential to be vigilant in verifying information and promoting honesty to counteract these dangers.

The serpent used this lie on Eve when it said, *"For Yahweh does know that in the day you eat thereof, your eyes shall be opened,"* **Genesis 4:5**. The enemy knew that deliberately disobeying Yahweh would never cause them to be like Him, but rather like them; demons.

Special Comment: Sadly, to say, the lies that I am presenting in this book, I have seen not only in the mouths of demons, but also in the tongues of those claiming to be religious and in atheists alike. I have seen many of those in Christianity, Islamic, Judaism, and other faiths, lie about their close walk with Yahweh, when they are hating their fellow man.

Lies of Fabrications: The lie of fabrication refers to the act of creating false information or stories with the intent to deceive others. It involves intentionally perverting the truth or completely inventing falsity. Fabrication can occur in various forms, ranging from spreading rumors and making up untrue claims to manipulating evidence or documents.

The danger of mendacity lies in the potential harm they can cause. When misleading intel is spread, it can lead to misunderstandings, conflicts, and even societal chaos. Fictitious lies can damage reputations, destroy relationships, and ruin lives. In some cases, they can have far-reaching consequences, affecting economies, politics, and public trust; just look at the effects most politicians have had on the lives of millions of people.

Moreover, lies of fabrication undermine the foundations of trust and credibility. They erode the fabric of society by creating an atmosphere of skepticism and suspicion. When people can no longer differentiate between truth and falsehood, it becomes harder to make informed decisions and engage in meaningful dialogue.

To combat the danger of lies of fabrication, it is crucial to promote critical thinking skills, fact-checking, and media literacy. Encouraging transparency and ethical communication can also help prevent the spread of fabricated lies. Ultimately, by challenging and exposing falsehoods, we can strive for a more truthful and trustworthy world.

Everything that the serpent said to Eve, was false! Something that you must know about all demons is this, all of the lies that I have described within this book, are in their mouths.

Due to Adam and Eve defiance toward Yahweh's only commandment to them, demons knew that they could fabricate false religions, in order to confuse people about who's the real and true living God.

Plagiarism: Plagiarism may seem like a harmless act, but its consequences are far from benign. The dangers of plagiarism lie in the harmful effects it can have on both individuals and society as a whole.

Firstly, from an academic standpoint, plagiarism undermines the integrity of the educational system. When students engage in plagiarism, they cheat themselves out of a valuable learning experience. It prevents them from developing critical thinking skills and the ability to express their own ideas.

Moreover, plagiarism can have severe repercussions for individuals. In academic and professional settings, it tarnishes one's reputation, credibility, and future opportunities. Being caught plagiarizing can lead to academic penalties such as failing grades, expulsion, or even being fired from a job. Additionally, the legal consequences of plagiarism can include lawsuits and hefty fines.

On a broader scale, plagiarism poses a threat to the progress of knowledge and stifles innovation. By copying and presenting others' work as their own, individuals impede the advancement of original ideas and hinder creativity.

In essence, the danger of plagiarism lies in its detrimental impact on education, personal integrity, and the overall intellectual growth of society. It is essential for individuals to understand and acknowledge the harmful effects of plagiarism, fostering a culture of originality and ethical conduct.

Through plagiarism, Satan could steal certain passages from the bible, and have it put into another book, and then, call it the truth or a pure work from the Creator. Or to create books that causes the people to worship the creation, instead of the creator.

Unveiling Satan's Manipulation: Plagiarism in Religious Texts
In a startling revelation, recent research suggests that Satan has cunningly utilized the tool of plagiarism to shape his own religious narrative.

Specifically, investigations have brought to light the numerous instances where Satan has brazenly pilfered details and passages from the Bible, strategically placing them within the Quran to deceive followers of Islam.

By twisting certain biblical stories, Satan has successfully sown seeds of confusion among Muslims. One egregious example is the rewriting of the account of Jesus' crucifixion. Unbelievably, the writers of the Quran were convinced by Satan to propagate a ruse, asserting that Jesus did not die on the cross. Instead, they claimed that Judas, the betrayer, took his place – an absurd fabrication intended to diminish the significance of Jesus' sacrifice.

It is crucial to emphasize that this discourse is not waged to offend any believers, but rather to expose the truth. As responsible individuals, it is our duty to share this knowledge. Come the day of judgment, if we fail to disclose these revelations, we risk being accused of withholding the truth. However, by presenting this revelation and individuals choosing to accept or reject it, we absolve ourselves from liability for their rejection.

The significance of this revelation lies in its potential to illuminate the insidious methods employed by Satan, urging us all to remain vigilant in our pursuit of truth, unity, and genuine spirituality.

Leading The Witness: Another form of lying is called: "**Leading the witness**." Leading the witness is a term commonly used in legal settings, particularly during a trial or deposition. It refers to a situation where a lawyer deliberately prompts or influences a witness to give a specific response that supports their case. However, leading the witness can have harmful effects on the accuracy and fairness of the judicial process.
One of the primary harmful effects of leading the witness is the potential distortion of the truth. By asking leading questions, attorneys can manipulate witnesses into providing answers that may not be entirely accurate or objective. This can undermine the integrity of the proceedings and result in a skewed portrayal of events.

Furthermore, leading the witness can also infringe upon the witness's autonomy and credibility. When witnesses are coerced or subtly influenced, it raises concerns about their ability to provide independent and reliable testimony. This can erode trust in the legal system and compromise the pursuit of justice.
To ensure a fair trial and uphold the principles of impartiality, it is crucial for attorneys to avoid leading the witness and instead allow witnesses to testify freely and without undue influence.

Unanimous Lying: What is unanimous lying and why is it dangerous? Unanimous lying refers to a situation in which a group of individuals collectively engage in spreading false information or deception while maintaining a united front. This consensus-based deception can have serious consequences and poses a significant threat to the fabric of truth and integrity in our society.

The danger of unanimous lying lies in the erosion of trust it causes. When a group of people unanimously perpetuates falsehoods, it becomes increasingly difficult to discern fact from fiction. This can lead to a breakdown in communication, polarize communities, and breed a culture of skepticism.
Moreover, unanimous lying can be exploited to manipulate public opinion, sway political discourse, and undermine democratic processes. It creates an environment where misinformation thrives, fostering division and hindering progress.

It is crucial to confront and expose unanimous lying whenever it occurs. Promoting transparency, fact-checking, and critical thinking are essential tools to combat this dangerous trend and uphold the principles of truth and accountability.

This is perhaps the devil most powerful and destructive weapons, because it has caused billions of people, throughout history, to echo certain lies. There are so many different religions, all proclaiming that their version of God is the only one, and everyone else is false, and they're willing to die for their belief. And while all of their founders claim to have the true messages and revelations from God almighty, none of their leaders died for their sins, except for in Christianity, Jesus Christ.

CASE FIVE: Spiritual Warfare

What you will learn in this chapter:

- demon intelligence
- About Spiritual Attacks
- different kinds of sins
- demons in the sins they're over
- should you cast out demons

"For we wrestle not against flesh and blood [other humans], but against principalities, against powers, against the rulers of the darkness of this world, against spiritual wickedness in high places," **Ephesians 6:12**.

Notice that the Bible says that our fight isn't with other humans [flesh and blood], but rather against devils! This is important because while our battle isn't against other people, demons will use them to war with us. As Christians, while our fight shouldn't be with other people, because many are willing to be used by them, we must learn how to deal with people who are governed by demons. With that being said, lets understand how demons are working through people and how to deal with them.

As I have already said, our fight shouldn't be with another human being, but more and more people are opening themselves up, to be used by them, so, as believers, we must be able to deal with such individuals. For instance, all spiritual attacks don't look like spiritual possessions. Oftentimes, spiritual attacks come in subtle forms, in ways that are not expected or noticed at first. Remember this, the primary weapon of the devil is deception, not aggression; just read how the serpent beguiled Eve!

Demons love to remain inconspicuous, if possible, while still causing chaos among the people. If demons openly revealed themselves, most people would immediately call upon Jesus [Yeshua], but if they can appear as a wolf in sheep's clothing, a spiritual guide or a guru, in the form of a mean boss, or a psychic, then the person is less likely to call upon the name of the Lord and to rebuke him or her in Jesus' name.

If they come in those forms I just listed, most will not fight them with the word of God, but rather, lower their guards. A person will not fight against something they don't see and know is demonic in nature. The duties of all demons are to get the person's eyes and focus upon the problems, hurt, pain, and so on, but never on the solution, which is Jesus Christ.

Most spiritual attacks will come from people. While demons are behind the attacks, most likely, if the person doesn't have the gift of discernment, they will not see them, but rather, the people who are doing the devil's business for him. Once again, if the demons were to attack a person physically, then he or she would call upon the name of the Lord God, and the demons would be defeated, but if they use someone close to them, say a spouse, family member, or another physical being, more than likely, they're going to fight against that person, whether with negative words or, physically, either way, the demons win!

To put things in perspective, two people are walking down a street, one is about ten feet ahead of the other one. The devil will throw a rock, hitting

the person who's in front and then, hide behind a tree, so when the individual who was struck, looks back to see who did it, they will only see the person behind them, not the one who actually threw it.
This is one of the major ways, demons are causing chaos within the world today, they're the driving force behind the world's problems, attacking people, but secretly hiding behind others.

<u>Something To Think About</u>: Yeshua was attack only once by Satan, during their time in the wilderness together, but all of the other times, he did it by using people; mostly through the religious folks. Demons are attacking the people of Yahweh, using other individuals. But we [believers] must continue to use our spiritual weapons, in order to overcome them.

Let's use the book of Joe/Job, when Satan attacked his animals [finances], faithful servants, and children, did Satan do it himself, or did he use Joe's enemies? The only time that Satan didn't use people to attack Joe, is when he fought against his physical body, causing boils to cover Joe from head to toes.

Let's look at the story of Moses, did demons attack Moses physically, or did they work through Pharoah and his soldiers to do so?

So, then how to deal with demons who are working within a person or people against you? Jesus revealed the coldness of their heart and how they were allowing the devil to use them [**John 8:43-45**], and so should we, whenever people are permitting demons to use them to fight against us. *"For we wrestle not against flesh and blood, but against principalities, powers, rulers of the darkness of this world, and spiritual wickedness in high places,"* **Ephesians 6:12**.

<u>Demon's Intelligence:</u>
Before we dive into our spiritual fights, I want you to understand this: both holy and unholy angels are far more intelligent than the smartest human that walked the face of the earth; outside of Yeshua. For instance, it is believed that Ainan Celeste Cawley had an IQ of 263, while the average IQ range between 90 to 109. It is believed that the average medical doctor has an IQ of 140 to 150.

While no one has been fortunate enough to give an angel an IQ test, if I was a gambling man, I would bet my entire life savings that an angel's IQ would be at least <u>**2,432.75**</u>. But how did I come up with such a number? In **1st Kings 6:23-28**, the height of the two Cherubim were '10 cubits,' which

equals 15ft. And their wingspan was the same, 15ft. While the average height for a man is 5'9in. Therefore, I subtracted the height of an angel from that of the average man: 15ft subtract 5'9" equals (9.25 or 9ft. and 3in.) And then I took the IQ of the smartest human and multiplied it times the 9.25, which equals= 2,432.75. It is possible that their IQ would be higher than this. Remember that angels have been around for thousands, or perhaps, millions of years.
My point is, without the indwelling of the Holy Spirit, you nor I could possibly outsmart them.

Next, they are far stronger than any human being who ever lived. One angel, killed 185,000 of the Assyrian in one night, **2nd Kings 19:35**. Think about this, when the United States of America drop two atomic bombs on Japan, on August 6th and 9th killing an estimated 214,000 people. If an angel were to killed in a two-day span, he would have killed 370,000 people.

Our best soldier in the United States of America couldn't have killed 185,000 soldiers in one night. My point is, our human strength is nowhere near the power of an angel. Therefore, without the Holy Spirit, they could kill thousands of people before you could count to one.

The bible says that they move like flashes of light [**Ezekiel 1:14**]. Light travels at _186,000_ miles per second. The diameter of our earth is 7,926 miles; this means that light can travel around our planet seven times in under two second, or about 1.5 second to be exact.

Q. How quick can a godly angel or a demon learn things?
A. I use this formula to understand how much quicker can something be learnt in spirit-time versus physical time.

1,000   1   One day is like a thousand years and vice-versal; so, then 1,000 years = 24 hours
   24   41.67   or 1 day. If you divide 1,000/24= 41.6666666667. Rounded off: 41.67

So, then, the average time to learn a language is three years, and by using this formula, 41.67/36 months
equals 1.1575 (1.16); so, then it would take an angel only one minute and sixteen seconds to become fluent in a language (1 minute and 16 seconds). Remember, this is spirit time, not physical time.

While the average Christian will be able to name only Lucifer as a bad angel, the bible actually mentions others, such as:

1. **Abaddon/Apollyon**, in **Revelation 9:1-11**. Whose name means *"destruction."* He is the lord over demon locusts, who will in the last days, torment all those who doesn't have the seal of Yahweh in their foreheads. The demon Abaddon/Apollyon and his army, will be released after the tribulation, or at the beginning of the great tribulation; the saints would have already been raptured. I do believe in pre-tribulation.

During this time, these demons, led by Abaddon will search and find anyone who doesn't have the seal of Yahweh written on their foreheads, and will hurt them for five months, but they're not permitted to kill them.

Something to Think About: It is possible for these demons not to be seen, but rather working through people, to inflict pain on others for five months.

2. **Belial**, found in **2nd Corinthians 6:15**; **Deuteronomy 15:9**; **1st Samuel 1:16, 10:27, 30:32**.
The children of Belial in **Deuteronomy 13:13**, love to hang among Yahweh's people and to cause doubt, in order to persuade them to serve other gods. Ergo, Lucifer/Satan has commissioned Belial with the assignment to entice humans to turn away from the true and living God, Yahweh.

Mystery Revealed: Any of the religions, claiming that the angel Gabriel, came and delivered them a message that contradicts the Holy Bible in anyway, is simply lying. He was only sent to: Daniel, Zacharias, and Mary, the mother of Yeshua. Though an angel did visit them, just not Gabriel; I will reveal who actually did.

There are other religions who have proclaimed that an angel from Yahweh, came to their founder, and has giving them a divine message for their followers; but now, I will reveal who this angel is and was, and is present in this present day: Belial!

The spirit of Belial is the demon over homosexuality, domestic violence, and rapists [**Judges 19:22-27**]. Belial is the demon behind greed and lust. The sons of Eli were known as the sons of Belial in [**1st Samuel 2:12-16**]. They used their position as priests to exhort from the people, the best of the meat brought before them for sacrifice. They were stealing the portion that belong to Yahweh. They were stealing the offerings of the Lord God.

The sons of Belial bear false witness against Naboth, in order to steal his vineyard in [**1st kings 21:10 & 13**], which called him to be killed. Therefore, the spirit of Belial is a lying spirit, and the lies that it tells, are the ones that are design to steal someone property and to have them killed.

In conclusion, the spirit of Belial is over these kinds of sins and actions:
- rapist   • homosexuals   • stealing offerings from the Lord God
- false witness   • premeditated murder   • greed
- false religions or occults   • domestic violence

So, then whenever you see these things at work, you know what evil spirit is behind them.

3. **Beelzebub**, this name used to be translated as [*lord of life*] but the Hebrews changed it to [*lord of flies or lord of dung*] found in **Matthew 12:24-27**. In the era of Yeshua, Beelzebub was taught to be the prince of demons. In the Old Testament, Beelzebul is reference as "Baal-Zebub," a Canaanite deity worshipped at Ekron.

"But the angel of the Lord said to Elijah the Tishbite, "Go up and meet the messengers of the king of Samaria and ask them, 'Is it because there is not God in Israel that you are going off to consult Baal-Zebub, the god of Ekron?" **2nd Kings 1:3**.

4. **Moloch**, found in **Leviticus 18:21**. This is another Canaanite deity associated in biblical sources with the practice of child sacrifice. The practice of Moloch is: children's sacrifice. The Canaanites would offer the young children as a sacrifice to Moloch.

Therefore, Lucifer/Satan has employed the demon Moloch to cause the people to offer their children/babies as a sacrifice [abortion], over to himself. Therefore, when you see a woman have an abortion or, a man or woman murdering their child or step-child, it is this demon who entice them to do so.

5. **Principalities**: The state, office, or authority of a prince. The position or responsibilities of a principal (as of a school). The territory or jurisdiction of a prince.
How the Demons of Principalities fight against the saints of Yahweh?

Fighting Against Our ***Prayers***: [**Daniel 10:12-14**]. The high-ranking demons, such as principalities, wars against the prayers of believers, trying to cause them to doubt that Yahweh hears them and secondly, that He's not going to honor their request. They don't want the saints to believe that, the fervent prayers of the righteous avails much [**James 5:16**].

Interesting Fact: Whenever a righteous person prays, and soon afterward, a certain person or small group of people begin fighting against that saint, as if they were actively fighting what the believer was praying for; this is a sign that that individual or group of people has been commissioned by a principality demon, to cause doubt within that believer, in order to stop their prayers from being answered.

Interesting Fact: Every country has a good and bad prince, is to influence that nation of people to do either good or evil. For instance, Michael is the prince over Israel [**Daniel 12:1**], but there's also an evil prince that Satan has set over it as well. When Daniel was praying, it took 21 days for him to receive the answer, because the evil prince of Persia [**Daniel 10:13**] fought against Gabriel, so Michael had to come and assist him in the fight, in order to deliver the message to Daniel. There also was a prince of Greece [**Daniel 10:20**].

The demonic princes are actively fighting against the prophets of Yahweh, because the true ones are able to release the perfect will of Yeshua within these last days, in which they don't want.

Fighting Against Our ***Faith***: *"Whenever you pray, believe that you will receive, and you shall have it,"* [**Mark 11:24**]. Therefore, it is the duty of principalities to war against a person's faith, by causing doubt. The Bible says that without faith, it is impossible to please Yahweh, because anyone who comes to Him must believe that He is, and that He's a rewarder to those who earnestly seeks Him, [**Hebrews 11:6**].

Ergo, whenever a person's faith in Yahweh ceases, not only will he or she stop coming to Him, but they will seek to either please themselves or other people. In addition, even if they receive a prophecy, they will not believe it.

Without faith, no mountain can be removed from their life. Life is extremely difficult for them because they don't have the faith to remove the mountain, they are forced to either go around it or to calm over it, which is nearly impossible. In order to achieve one's dreams in life, he or she must believe that they can do it.

Fighting Against Our ***Works*** for Yahweh: [**James 2:17**]. Whenever you see a person who claim to be a follower of Christ Jesus, but their deeds are everywhere except of doing Yahweh's business, it is due to the demon under principalities are actively fighting against that person.

Principality demons promote things like genocide, systemic or institutional racism, sex trade workers.

6. **Powers**: Ability to act or produce an effect. Legal or official authority, capacity, or right. Possession of control, authority, or influence over others. A controlling group.

How the Demons of Power fight against people?
Every law-makers, that create laws that are contrary to the word of Yahweh, is under the influence of the power demons. But they just don't manipulate and control law makers, but any who possesses power to affect the lives of many people. For example, whenever you see price gouging, it is due to the power demons, it is their task to oppress people.

Also, it is a distraction, causing the people to complain and dislike those who are behind the unnecessary increases, instead of turning their hearts and faces toward the Lord God, who's able to bless in-spite of high inflations. In the book of **Revelation 6:5-6**, the price of food is going to increase so immensely, that a person must work a complete day is to purchase wheat and or barley.

All autocrats, militaries and or polices who break the law or abuse people, is governed by demons of power.

These kinds of demons love to work in churches where the pastors are hirings, or its ran by deacons, which is totally unscriptural. The entire chapter of **Matthew 23**, exposes how both the Scribes and Pharisees were being controlled by the power demons.

• They promote themselves or have someone who Yahweh hasn't pointed, to positions within church or the synagogue. The Scribes and Pharisees were not prophets and therefore, had no right to sit in such a seat of power and authority [**Matthew 23:1**]. Lucifer has assigned certain people to infiltrate the church, to support that church with large sums of money, in order to gain the attention of the pastors there, and to become close.
And to use their gifts there, so that the pastor will promote him or her to a high position, and once there, will begin discovering ways to incorporate

the doctrine of devils, or blackmail the pastor if he doesn't comply with their demands, or to destroy that church. Later, I will reveal Satan's secret agent.

Therefore, whenever you see a religious person telling the truth, but they themselves will not practice it, he or she is under the power demon's influence. In addition, the power demon's controls and destroys people's lives through illegal drug [including marijuana] and alcohol addiction.

7. **Rulers of Darkness Demons**: are the demons that try to control all people through sins. Therefore, they're assigned by Satan himself, to keep people sinning, and to die in them. **Comment:** Just as Lucifer said, "**I Will**," five times, I have found five areas where sin can exist. And because 666 is the mark of the beast, each category has 18 different sins: 6+6+6=18.

6+6+6= 18
2nd Tim. 3:1-5

1. lovers of self [selfish]
2. covetous
3. boasters
4. proud
5. blasphemers
6. disobedient to parents
7. unthankful
8. unholy
9. trucebreakers
10. false accusers
11. incontinent
12. fierce
13. despisers of those that are good

14. traitors
15. heady
16. high-minded
17. lovers of pleasure More than lovers of God
18. form of godliness But denying the power

6+6+6= 18
Galatians 5:19-21

1. Adultery
2. Fornication
3. Uncleanness
4. Lasciviousness
5. Idolatry
6. Witchcraft
7. Hatred
8. Variance
9. Emulations
10. Wrath
11. Strife
12. Sedition
13. Heresies

14. Envying
15. Murder
16. Drunkenness
17. Reveling

18. Unmerciful

Thereof
6+6+6= 18

1. Stealing
2. Lying
3. Fearful/cowardly
4. Bestiality
5. Slothful
6. Racism
7. Hateful Words
8. Rejoicing with Evil
9. Not doing good
   When you know to
10. Bitterness
11. Teaching False
    Doctrine
12. False witness
13. Evil thoughts
14. Jealousy
15. Unbelief
16. Unforgiveness
17. Rapist
18. Idol Time

6+6+6= 18
wrong because the
Romans 1:18-32
their own body
1. They subdued the truth; God revealed it
2. They knew God but wouldn't glorify Him
testimony
3. They weren't thankful
4. They became futile in their imagination
or selling them
5. Their hearts were darkened
like
6. Claiming to be wise, they became fools
7. Changed the glory of God, into men & animal
8. God gave them over to their own lust
9. They changed the truth of God into a lie
10. They worshipped the universe, not God
11. God gave them over to homosexuality
12. God gave them over to reprobate mind

6+6+6= 18

1. Cannibalism
2. Pedophilia
3. Greed
4. Gluttony
5. Carousing
6. Complaining
7. Cowardice
8. Denying Christ
9. Desiring Praise/Worship

10. Divorce
11. Hypocrisy

12. Jesting Inappropriately
13. Judging (Condemning)
14. Prostitution
15. Blackmail
16. Swearing
17. Provoking someone to anger
18. Worrying

This last category is

person is destroying

[1st Corinthians 3:17]
Will harm your

1. Tobacco Products●
2. Illegal Drugs/ taking

3. Marijuana and such

4. Self-Injury

13. Malicious   14. Breaking the Sabbath Day
15. Rumormonger/whisperer
16. Backbiter   17. Haters of God
18. Inventors of evil

All sins can be forgiven, except for the sin of blasphemy against the Holy Spirit/Ghost.
Sin can be put into five categories, and they are:

Category 1: Sin
A person has failed
short in their walk
with God or a
with a person

Category 2: Transgression
The person was face with
a choice to do good or evil,
but due to their feeling,
choose to do wrong

Category 3: Iniquities

Doing wrong and plan
on doing addition evil
and encourages others
to do wickedness

Category 4: Willful

A person who knew
God and knows what's right
in his sight, but has turned from
Him and is now doing wicked
things

Category 5: Unforgivable

A person who declares that Jesus' spirit
is unclean or proclaims that he cast
out demons by the spirit of Beelzebub.

8. **Spiritual Wicked In High Places**: are the demons that work among those who are in government, presidents, CEO over large Incorporations, heads of the entertainment business, news owners, movies and music producers, and so on. Any person who has power to affect the lives of multitudes of people, are where these demons seek to have hegemony.

In conclusion: from the highest to the lowest ranking demons:
• Satan/Lucifer   • spiritual wicked in high places demons   • rulers of the darkness demons   • power demons   • principalities demons

9. **Demon of Fear**

"For Yahweh has not given us the spirit of fear, but of power, and of love, and of a sound mind," **2nd Timothy 1:7**. Fear isn't just a feeling, but rather a real spirit!

The spirit of fear possesses a haunting power, an insidious force that silently weaves through the fabric of our lives, corroding the person from within. It knows no boundaries, infiltrating the person's mind and heart, destroying the individual's life piece by piece.

Like a vicious apex predator, the spirit of fear preys upon the person's hopes and dreams, paralyzing them with its deadly grip. It whispers lies of inadequacy, convincing the individual that they're not worthy of love, respect, or success. It manipulates a person's thoughts, constructing a prison of self-doubt and insecurity.

With each passing moment, the spirit of fear eats away at the person's confidence, strangling their ambitions and causing an erosion of their true potentials. It robs them of opportunities, forcing him or her to live a life confined within the confines of their comfort zones. It shackles and enslave their creativity and suffocates their desires, leaving them stagnant and unfulfilled.

Worse yet, the spirit of fear, like a predator, carefully studies the person and learns what they fear the most, and then, gather those things, and bring them into that individual's life; turning their life into a living nightmare. And once their ephialtes begins, the spirit of fear will fill their heart with anxiety and worry, poisoning their relationships and robbing them of joy.

It isolates the person, as they become too afraid to take risks, too terrified to let others in; and in some situations, causing them to behave like someone who's suffering from paranoid personality disorder. It blinds their perceptions, distorting reality and blinding them to the beauty that's surround.

Just listen to what Joe/Job said, *"The thing that I greatly feared the most has come upon me,"* **Job 3:24**. You see, it was the thing he'd greatly feared actually happened to him. So then, before Joe lost his animals [finances], ten children, most of his servants [employees], and health, he was allowing fear to enter his heart. So, then it didn't matter how much he was praying and making burnt offerings for his children, because his own fears did cancel those things out.

Special Comment: if you're allowing the spirit of fear to govern over your life, and you are a born-again Christian, you have the power and authority in Yeshua's name, to stop it today, right now!

Fear will chase a person like a lion pursue after its prey. During the chase, it will lead you into places that you don't want to go or, be in. And if you exhaust all or most of your energy in fleeing, whenever it catches you, and eventually it will, you will not have enough strength to defend yourself, and it will prevail and become a dictator over your life.
But it will not stop at controlling you, but it will insist that you teach your insecurities to your love ones and close allies.

Internal Fears→ •Self-Doubts •Insecurities

•Focusing On Setbacks •Trying Instead of Doing

•Depression •Low Self-Esteem (Character)

•Suicidal Ideation •Focusing on Dying

•Low Self-Esteem (Appearance & Character) •I'm too old now

External Fears→ •Feeling Like they can't escape their Environment

•Feeling Rejected/Abandon •Accepting Destructive Criticism from Haters •Verbal Abuse •Physical Abuse •Sexual Abuse •Abandonment

Imaginary Fears→ These are the fears that a person believes something negative will occur to them somewhere in the future or, something that has happened to them and they believe it will happen again.

Common Fears→ There are fears that I refer to as "common or natural fears," which involves the person being afraid of some kind of wild or dangerous animal, going into a dangerous neighborhood, having a gun or knife pointed at them, having surgery, etc. And while these fears can trigger the same kinds of emotions as the other three, most of the time they're temporary or occurring only at that moment, then afterwards, a thing of the past.

But what are the main internal enemies that prohibit a person's greatness?

The thing that seems fearful will always appear to be bigger and much stronger than the person; and if they're not willing to face their fears and have a strategic plan to defeat it, then it will drive them to perilous places and cause him or her to make decisions that are harmful for them. And because the individual has allowed the fear to chase them, and they have exhausted their strength in running, when they face their fear, they will not be able to prevail against it.

The Strength of Fear→ Fear gets its strength for the person's own self-doubts, insecurities, revenge, and so on. The stronger the person becomes, so will their fears too.

The Attacks of Fear:

Lack of Courage: One of the first things that fear does is it attacks the person's courage, and once their courage is weaken, it causes the individual to become a coward; avoiding just about any kind of confrontation or when they do decide to handle it, they wait until the situation or condition is almost out of hand. The fear will drive the person back to where they're most comfortable and safe. Instead of becoming the hero, fear transforms the individual into a victim of circumstances.

Hiding Instead of Facing: While all of us [human-beings] have some secrets that we want to keep buried or out of view, people who live in fear are known for concealing many of their errors and the dispute with this is, when confronted with their mistake, they are known for blaming others instead of taking responsibilities for their own actions. The greater the fear, the more enormous the person's inner battles will be.

It's difficult helping someone who's fearful, because they're reluctant to stand and fight. Their own fears continue to remind them how they fail the last time and the great pain that's associated with it. Fear prevents the person from trusting just about anyone, due to their sensitive information being divulged, but secret sins will always bring about secret battles. And it's almost impossible to overcome secret battles because the person isn't able to tell anyone what they are going through.

Going Back: Fear causes the person to return back to a hostile situation or condition. Even when they know that the problem will not change, they will accept an abnormal condition or situation as normal [it is what it is!]. Fear will cause a woman to remain in an abusive relationship with a man, for fear of not being able to provide for her-self [insufficient funds], family, and so on. She will not leave her abuser, for fear of not finding anyone to replace him. For she's convinced that she isn't pretty enough for someone else, too overweight, etc.

For you have not received the spirit of bondage again to fear: but you have received the Spirit of adoption whereby we cry, Abba Father." **Roman 8:15.**

10. **The Spirit of Error** [1st **John 4:6**] primarily duty is to cause people to be full of repeated mistakes throughout their life. Ergo, the moment the child's mother decides not to abort her unborn child, the spirit of error begins making pernicious plans for that child's future while still in the womb. But in order to make its abominable plan work against the unborn child, the evil spirit must have carefully studied the behavior of its parents, knowing the things that constantly caused them to error in their past, and the things that are currently failing at. By understanding those things, then the evil spirit can effectively begin it aggressive attack when the child enters into this world.

For instance, when there was a famine in the land, Abraham went down to Egypt and there, he lied to Pharoah, saying that Sarah was only his sister, instead of confessing that she was really his wife, [**Genesis 12:10-20**]; so, did his son Isaac, when there was a famine in the land, he also lied [**Genesis 26:1-11**] to Abimelech about Rebekah being his wife. Rebekah told Jacob to deceive to his father in order to obtain the birth-right [**Genesis 27:6-10**].

Jacob lied to his father Isaac, in order to obtain the birth-right [**Genesis 27:14-25**]. I could continue with this, but I think that you understand by now who the spirit of error knew how to attack their lineage whenever things they faced some difficulties.

The dictionary defines an error as an act or condition of ignorant or imprudent deviation from a code of behavior. An act involving an unintentional deviation from truth or accuracy, and an act through ignorance, deficiency, or accident departs from or fails to achieve what should be done.

Through ignorance, does the spirit of error obtains its strength. Therefore, it is the duty of this evildoing spirit is to keep a person oblivious about Yahweh and what He has said about them, who they are, and how to prosper in life. Once a person is overcome by this evil spirit, mistakes, doubt, depression, and low self-esteem will flow through their lives like a heart that pumps blood throughout a person's body.

The Spirit of Bondage prohibited or restricts a person's hand from producing a harvest. A person can plant much, but they will only reap back a little; seem like the curse cannot and will not be broken over their life.
Q. *"How do you detach yourself from the Spirit of Bondage?"*
A. By accepting the Holy Spirit into their heart. *"Now the Lord is the Spirit; and where the Spirit of the Lord is, there is liberty,"* **2ⁿᵈ Corinthians 3:17**. *"Therefore, if the Son makes you free, you shall be free indeed,"* **John 8:36**.

11. **Familiar spirits**
Question: *"What are familiar spirits?"*

Answer: The word familiar is from the Latin familiaris, meaning a *"household servant,"* and intended to express the idea that sorcerers had spirits as their servants ready to obey their commands. Those attempting to contact the dead, even to this day, usually have some sort of spirit guide who communicates with them. These are familiar spirits.

Lev. 19:31; 20:6, 27; and **Deut. 18:9-14** refer to "mediums and familiar spirits" and forbids being involved with them, as they are an abomination to the Lord. The medium was one who acted as a "go-between" to supposedly contact or communicate with the dead, but in reality, they were contacting demons who convinced the mediums that they were "familiar" and could be trusted and believed. The practices associated with mediums and familiar spirits were banned in Israel, and the punishment for practicing such things, was death.

Familiar spirits, known to be the most perilous types of demons, possess an inherent danger due to their close connection with a family's lineage. These eerie entities are often recognized as long-standing members of a household, frequently seen and well known to all. Their presence transcends time, entwining themselves across generations, making them even more formidable adversaries.

Unlike other demonic entities that may come and go over a period of time, familiar spirits remain well acquainted with the individuals they haunt. Their intimate knowledge of a family's inner workings grants them unparalleled power and influence over their victims.

Having inhabited the lives of countless ancestors, familiar spirits exploit the vulnerability that comes from such extensive familiarity. They exploit the deepest fears and desires that have been passed down from one generation to the next, creating a sinister grip that is virtually impossible to break.

Caution must be exercised when encountering these malevolent beings. Their historical ties and unholy connection to the bloodline make familiar spirits a force to be reckoned with, demanding the utmost vigilance and strength to overcome.

For instance, within that family's lineage, the person's great, great, grandfather was an alcoholic. And let's say that his son was one also. And suppose the great, great, grandfather dies of alcohol poisoning, due to drinking and his son as well, that familiar spirit hasn't left that family, just because the great, great, grandfather and son have both died of alcohol, but rather will remain within that same family's lineage, trying to convince the remaining of their descendants to partake of alcohol, and die as the previous ones.

While the other evil spirits will try to remain inconspicuous within a family, familiar spirits will not, because it has been a part of that particular family for so long, throughout many generations, that it doesn't feel the need to conceal itself, but rather is accepted and adopted into that family as normal behavior, instead of, a dysfunctional one.

In this next section, you will learn how a particular spirit, is linked to serval other things and therefore, if you allow that spirit into your life, you can expect other things to follow.

Lucifer's Spirit: [Iniquities] Self-Glory→ Pride→ Prevarication→ Self-Deception→ Folly→ Stealing→ Destroying→ Murdering

Spirit of Legion: Crying Out Strangely→ Supernatural Strength→ Cutting Themselves→ Living in The Graveyard→ Attempting Suicide Multiple Times→ Forming from the Mouth

Unclean Spirit: Diseases→ Sickness→ Make Loud Noises→ Lacking Self-Control→ Self-Infliction→ Suicidal→ Dwelling Among Dead Things

Victim's Evil Spirit: Rejection→ Loneliness→ Self-Pity→ Misery→

Depression→ Despair→ Self-Condemnation→ Self-Hate

Lying Spirit: [The Tongue] Compulsive Liars → Exaggeration→ Gossip→ Criticism→ Idle Words→ False Prophecies→ Speaking Curses→ Speaking False Visions

Deceiving Spirit: Sophistry→ False Enlightenment→ Indecision→ Prevarication→ Disobedience→ Shame→ Hiding→ Accuser/Blaming

Ruler Of Darkness: Unknown Darkness→ Fear→ Anger→ Hate→ Regrets→ Suffering→ Offense→ Revenge→ violence

Obesity Spirit: Craving Unhealthy Foods→ Unhealthy Drinks→ Overindulgence→ Selfishness→ Greediness

Sexual Demon: [Lust of the Eyes] Viewing Only Fans→ Viewing Porn→ Spiritual Adultery→ Deviant Fantasies→ Masturbation→ Nymphomania/Satyriasis→ Engaging in Prostitution→ Orgies

People who deal with a lustful sexual demon is likely to have dreams about having sexual intercourse with a complete stranger, as so long as the person is attractive and wanting to have sex; not knowing that its nothing but a demon, disguised as an attractive person.

Dream Of Mine: I saw a wicked person and immediately discerned who it was. As this wicked man entered into a house in a well-kept neighborhood, I secretly followed him and saw what was inside. Two men and women were having sexual intercourse, and during this process, two evil spirits ascend up from the earth, and entered into the women. When I saw this discussing act, immediately I left and I saw my deceased mother, and two of my sisters.

I asked my mother and older sister did they see what was happening, and they said yes, but my younger sister said no. Then I explained to my mother what I saw within the house, and about the evil spirits. Then she said, "_The devil didn't want you to see that_!"

Then an audible voice said to me, "_Go back in the house and rebuke the whores_!" I was somewhat afraid because I knew that the evil man was a high-ranking demon. Then I said, "Lord, if you be with me, then I will go." Once assured, I went back. I entered the house and rebuked the whores and the high-ranking spirit was furious. I left the house and while on the top step of the house, I saw two evil shadow demons coming toward me. I looked up to heaven and said, "Lord, you told me to rebuke the whores, and I did.

Now these two evil spirits are about to attack me." Then an audible voice said, "I am with you!" Then I looked to my left and saw a mighty angel, dressed in pure white with a sword. And with the sword, he cut the two shadow demons in half. When the high-ranking evil spirit saw this, he released a wave of demons against me.

Then I looked up into the sky and saw Yeshua, standing in front of a host of angels and they descended on my right side. Then Yeshua pointed His finger at the demons that were sent to harm me, and immediately, at lightspeed, around seven of them attacked those demons, and destroyed them all. Then I awaken.

Dream Interpretation:
●The evil man was the antichrist. Remember his name means: against Christ, instead of Christ, oppose to Christ. Whatever that's in a person's life, that is taking Yahweh's place, is a form of antichrist.

Comment: Instead of trying to discover the identity of the antichrist, one should see how much of his spirit is in them. What things has replaced God in their life?

●The house represented myself, sadly to say. In the past, I was like so many of men, addicted to porn. But I had gotten delivered from it, but the dream was revealing to me that Satan was planning on leading me back to it.

●you don't have to physically be having sex with someone in order for it to be adultery. Yeshua said, "If you look upon a woman [person], and lust after them, you have committed adultery [spiritual adultery] already with that individual in your heart.

●Me seeing the couples having sex represented my past addiction to viewing porn. Whenever a person commits adultery or fornication, he or she is opening themselves for the invasion of a demon.

● Me walking out of the house, refusing to watch such an act, revealed that I had stopped or quit watching it, in which I did.

- Asking my mother and older sister were they able to see it, in which they did, represent that, in two major ways, I was able to see how I was being tricked into watching porn, even when in the past I swore not to watch it again.

My younger sister couldn't see; which represented that Satan wanted to attack a blind spot on me. For me to see something, that while appearing to be innocent or not so harmful, but would be actually dangerous for me to view, and that thing would plant a seed within my mind, so I could return to porn. For instance, viewing a commercial that showed women half dress or a sitcom, where couples are engaging in sex, while appearing to be innocent, could be dangerous for someone recovering from porn addiction. The bible says, "*Give no place to the devil*," **Ephesians 4:27**. Therefore, I stopped watching anything that contained sexual content, closing all doors was of necessity.

- The voice telling to return and rebuke the whores represented Yahweh, letting me know that I had to face my demons, not run from them, and that He was with me.

My obedience to Yahweh was my breakthrough. Yeshua wanted me to stand up against it, but using His word, and I did.

- Me telling my mother about seeing the demons enter into the women, and she said, "Satan didn't want you to see that," represented that the devil didn't want Yahweh to reveal that kind of information, because the demons knew that not only would I stop watching porn, but I would write this book and reveal it to you [the reader], letting you know that every time you view porn, or masturbate to it, a demon is released into your life, as you're pleasuring yourself.

Remember the story in **Genesis 6**, when the sons of God [fallen angels] came and had sexual relations with the women. Whenever you lust after someone, whether it is a man or woman, I can assure you that a demon is entering you. I saw it with my own eyes in the spirit.

Special Comment: The women represent the weaker vessels; demons enter in the areas where the person is more vulnerable. I have written this because I don't want you to think that they can just enter into women, no, they're entering in the areas of your life where you're giving in to sin.

- The two shadow demons were the spirits that where in the couples having sex. They wanted to enter me, but couldn't. Yeshua just don't want to be with a person, but rather to live in their heart.

- The angel taking the sword, and cutting the demon shadows in half represent, I must use the word of God, the sword of the spirit to defeat them. Please remember that it's not enough to quote the word to demons, you must live it also.

- The many evil spirits I seen on my left represented; Jesus said that whenever a demon leaves a person and return, it brings seven other spirits, wickeder than itself, and they enter into that person. Now, if a person gets delivered again [demons casted out of that person] but they return to the previous sin, if each one of those spirits, go and gather eight more, that will equal 64 demons. And if each one of those 64 go and gather 8, it would equal 512 demons. The point is, every time you get delivered from something evil, if you don't stay away from that thing, then it will go and gather additions demons, is to help it fight against you.

What I was witnessing in the dream is my Lord God's goodness and mercy, because all of those demons were representing the many times that I had been delivered, but returned back to that sin, and those demons when and gather additional ones, so they could eventually, possess me.

- We oftentimes look up to the sky for Yeshua, but He's inside of us, if you're a believer. He is in the midst of believers. The seven angels represent: perfection, rest. Yeshua wanted me to enter into His rest and that no weapon, whether from the devil or from one of his children, can destroy me.

Spirit of Error: Fellowshipping with Toxic People→ Giving in To Peer-Pressure→ Unrealistic Fantasies→ Unrealistic Expectations→ Easily Duped→ Easily Confused→ Embraces Falsehood→ Spreads Misinformation

Spirit of Baal Worship: They worship Baal when they wanted to be blessed financially. The children of Israel worship it when they made a golden calf [bull]. While in today's world, the people might say, people no longer are worshipping such a false deity, but they would be wrong. At the New York Stock Exchange, there is a bull there! People want a "Bull Market," representing that they Stock Market is going up.

Casting Out Demons

Sceva, who is identified as "a Jewish chief priest (**Acts 19:14**) had seven sons; and one day they decided to cast out evil spirits like they heard Jesus had done and Paul was currently doing. As they attempted to cast them out, the demon replied, *"Jesus I know, and Paul I know, but who are you?"* (**Acts 19:15**). Then the man who had the unclean spirit, attacked the seven sons of Sceva, overpowering and causing injuries to them; and they ran out of the house nude.

My strong advice is this, a person should never try to copy what someone else has been called to do, unless they themselves have been empowered to do likewise. Secondly, when dealing with demons, the person must be filled with the Holy Spirit. And finally, the person should know or be familiar with demons, by studying and understanding their nature. As Christians, we should never be afraid of them, but it's wise to know as much as possible about our enemies. The strength of all enemies lies in the ignorance of not knowing their capabilities.

True Story: In Jesus' name, I have personally experienced casting out demons on three separate occasions. I firmly believe that while demons should not be feared, they must be taken seriously. After successfully casting out a demon from a person, I make it a point to direct them where to go, as this is crucial to me. However, there was one instance during a church service where I failed to do so. I cast the demon out of one individual, but neglected to give it a specific destination.

As a result, the spirit of fear left that person and entered another who happened to be just twenty feet away. It was only later, when this second woman approached me, that I became aware of the transfer. Therefore, I strongly suggest that before casting out demons, it is essential to pray over the people nearby to prevent any unwanted transference, and then bravely cast out the demons without hesitation.

Important Intel: When casting out an evil spirit, you cannot send them into hell, because it's not their time to suffer there yet. Only Yahweh can send them there, no human!

CASE SIX: *The Children Of Demons*

"Why is my language not clear to you? Because you are unable to hear what I say. You belong to your father, the devil, and you want to carry out

your father's desires. He was a murderer from the beginning, not holding to the truth, for there is no truth in him. When he lies, he speaks his native language, for he is a liar and the father of lies. Yet because I tell the truth, you do not believe me!" **John 8:43-45 NIV**.

Yeshua is revealing to us, exactly who are the children of the devil, not by flesh and blood, but by soul-ties. Satan is a father to these groups of people: all lies, children of the disobedience, people who have a form of godliness, and false religions around the world.

Satan as a father over religious people: Yeshua clearly tells the religious people in that era, that they're were of their spiritual father, the Devil himself, and that's why they weren't able to understand nor hear him. Being religious doesn't imply that the person has a relationship with Yeshua. Millions of people, around the world, attend church services, sing in the choir, teach and preach sermons, and yet, don't have a personal relationship with Him. Satan had blinded their mind in such a way, that they believed that in killing Yeshua, God himself would be pleased with them.

The Children of Belial:
"Certain men, the children of Belial, are gone out from among you, and have withdrawn the inhabitants of their city, saying, *"Let us go and serve other gods, which you have not known."* **Deuteronomy 13:13**.

Belial, the malevolent demon of ancient lore, wields an insidious power over humanity through his deceptive offspring. Known for their ability to entice and deceive, the children of Belial have played a pivotal role in luring people away from the path of truth. Their wicked influence has led countless individuals astray, causing them to abandon the worship of the true and living God.

In the present day, this dark force continues to manipulate unsuspecting souls through false religious practices. Unbeknownst to those who partake, Belial exercises control over these counterfeit faiths, masquerading as the divine. How tragic it is that those who believe themselves to be devout followers of the Almighty are unknowingly worshipping the very essence of wickedness.

Beware, for all false deities and religions in our world today operate under the sinister dominion of Belial. Like a tangled web, his control stretches far and wide, ensnaring those who seek spiritual solace. It is imperative to remain vigilant, for only by recognizing this deceit and being led by the Holy Spriit, can we free ourselves from the clutches of darkness and embrace the truth.

The children of Belial wanted to have sex with other men {homosexuals}[22], and when they didn't have access to the man, an older man sent out his concubine to them, in which they raped her [25] and abused her throughout the night, and at dawn they let her go. **Judges 19**.

The old man, cognizant of the sinister desires that consumed them, believed he could strike a dark bargain. Desperation fueled his actions, as he sought to protect the stranger under his roof and those he held dear from their twisted lusts.

With trembling hands and a heavy heart, the old man approached the wicked sons of Belial, his voice laced with fear and desperation. He proposed an unimaginable exchange - his innocent daughter and faithful concubine, offered as sacrificial lambs to satiate their depravity.

Yet, even this grisly offering failed to satiate their insatiable derangement. Savagery overtook reason and morality. Ignoring the abhorrent nature of their actions, they pounced upon the trembling concubine, raping her repeatedly, until no strength remained with them. In this repugnant act of assault, darkness descended upon the hapless woman, an innocent victim of unparalleled depravity.

The children of Belial, denied their homosexual act, grew furious as their twisted desires remained unfulfilled. Their anger, a manifestation of their corrupted souls, brewed like a tempest, ready to unleash havoc upon all who crossed their path.

The children of Belial brought great evil in Gibeah, and they were to be put to death for their wickedness, **Judges 20:13**.

The weight of their sins demanded a just punishment, as their heinous acts left an indelible mark upon the very fabric of Gibeah. The decree echoed with unwavering resolve: the agents of such unrelenting evil were to face the ultimate consequence. For their crimes against humanity, the sons of Belial were doomed to meet their fate at the hands of justice. Thus, the sword of retribution hung in the air, ready to strike down the vile perpetrators, as Gibeah braced itself to witness the eradication of darkness and the restoration of righteousness.

Now the sons of Eli were sons of Belial; they knew not the Lord, **1st Samuel 2:12**. The sons of Eli were stealing the offerings, the very thing that belonged to Yahweh and having sex with the women in the church. Eli, a revered priest ordained by God, was widely recognized for his righteousness and devotion. However, his sons, Hophni and Phinehas, unfortunately earned a reputation quite contrary to their father's virtue. They were labeled as the sons of Belial, a term signifying their wickedness and defiance towards God.

Their transgressions extended beyond mere misbehavior, as they shamelessly exploited their positions within the church. Not only did Hophni and Phinehas brazenly pilfer offerings that rightfully belonged to God, but they also engaged in sinful acts of fornication with the women in their congregation.

Such profound disrespect towards the divine greatly angered God, leading to dire consequences. As a consequence of their heinous actions, God decreed the destruction of both Hophni and Phinehas, a stark reminder of the consequences faced by those who defy and dishonor the Almighty. Eli, torn between loyalty to his sons and his devotion to God, was left to grapple with the devastating repercussions of their grievous choices.

They said he cursed the king and God, so the people stoned him to death, **1st Kings 21:13**.

In a wicked scheme orchestrated by Jezebel, the sons of Belial were summoned to execute a sinister plan against the innocent man, Naboth. Fueled by greed and a thirst for power, they fabricated false charges against him, aiming to seize his prized land so Jezebel could give it to her husband, king Ahab.

With deceptive tongues, they accused Naboth of blaspheming both God and the king. These groundless allegations, backed by their unholy determination, led to his unjust condemnation and subsequent execution. It was a ruthless ploy, designed to strip Naboth of his rightful inheritance and enrich those driven by malevolence. However, this act of treachery served as a chilling testament to the depths of evil humanity can sink to when driven by a covetous heart and an insatiable desire for control.

In conclusion: We are about to witness the spirit of Belial working through his children, as I have just revealed to you, but this time, on a much higher scale, because this kind of behavior is about to become prevalent. Especially within these next two years. The current date is January 31, 2024. In another book of mine, I will be revealing end-times prophecies.

CASE SEVEN   *Season Of Attacks*

After reading this chapter, you should be able to:

• know what season you're currently being attacked in

The bible says that after Satan ended his attacks on Yeshua while in the wilderness, he departed, but for only a season [**Luke 4:13**]; this implies that he was coming back. But after he fought against Yeshua in the wilderness, he no longer came in his spirit form, but rather attacking him through God's own creation, humans. Satan used religious leaders to war against Jesus.

In this section, I will cover the most sixteen common attacks that demons are using against people. None of these attacks from demons are in a chronological order.

Season One Attack One: *Sexual Lust*

The term "Old Flame" refers to someone with whom the person has had a past sexual relationship with. If the person is currently married to someone and then suddenly, a sexual mental image from their past, that they had with someone, before they got married comes to mind, it's because a demon has put that evil thought in that person's mind. It is hoping that he or she continues to entertain that sexual experience, because that demon has two things that it wants to do within their life.

First Thing: It wants the person to imagine how good the sex was and how well they look, so they will remain in adultery. *Second Thing*: At the very moment that demon brought that mental image to his or her mind, the image of that person in whom the demon brought to their mind at that moment, was currently experiencing some kind of spiritual attack from other demons, and that demon wants that person, who they brought the image to, to be attacked also by those demons as well.

For example: John Doe is married to Jane Doe. While watching a movie, Jane Doe sees a handsome and well-built man, who reminds her of an old boyfriend she used to be romantically involved with. And at that moment, a demon brought Jane a mental image of her ex-boyfriend, whose name is Joe. Instead of Jane rebuking the sexual thought and the resisting the demon who brought it, she permits the deviate fantasy to continue, and eventually, makes up an excuse to take a shower in order to masturbate. But what she doesn't know, at that very moment, Joe has been suffering from major depressive disorder and is contemplating on whether to end his life are not; in addition, he's suffering from schizophrenia.

As she fantasized about her and Joe's sexual encounter, while pleasuring herself in the bathroom, the demons that is vexing Joe at that very moment, some of them leaves him and enters into Jane's home and immediately comes to her. And while they may not be able to enter and possess her at that very moment, nevertheless, they compel her to lust after Joe again.

Because she doesn't repent, whenever her and her husband get into an argument, the depression that was vexing Joe, now is able to vex her; causing her negative emotions to run wild, and to eventually, entertain thoughts of suicide.

Soon after, she will start to hear voices within her head, voices that will accuse her husband of infidelity, even when she has no strong evidence of it. Symptoms of paranoid personality disorder will begin to manifest itself. While in the past, she was able to think clearly, but now her thinking is distorted and feel somewhat blah when attempting to communicate with her husband.

And every time she fantasizes about Joe, sexually, more and more demons make their way into their home. Now the demons are able to affect her body by disrupting the sexual intimacy between her and her husband. The only time she will be able to have pleasure in that way, is when she's thinking about Joe. But the demons will not stop at Joe, all of her past sexual encounters will begin to proliferate, causing her to reminisce about her past sexual experiences; even if she has watched porn, she will begin to imagine being with one of them.

Important Intel: Most people in the church-world are familiar with the term "familiar spirits" but not with what I call as "strange or unfamiliar spirits." A strange or unfamiliar spirits are the evil demons that aren't associated in your family. For instance, if nobody in your family is a porn star or a prostitute, and then, someone engages in such a thing, this would be known as a strange or unfamiliar spirit, because it doesn't run in your family.

This is why it is of necessity for a person to be delivered and made free by the precious blood of Yeshua, so they aren't bringing unclean spirits and or strange/unknown spirits into their new relationship.

Inconclusion: Allowing and entertaining sexually fantasies is not just dangerous because its adultery [**Matthew 5:27-28**], but also, because it will elicit whatever demons that the other person is currently battling with, to enter into the one whose lusting after them.

Season One Attack Two: *I Can't Forgive You*

Dave's actions over the years have left Jill deeply hurt and betrayed. His infidelity, getting two other women pregnant, lying about his whereabouts, unable to keep a job, causing her to have two miscarriages due to great stress and physical violence, going to bars and hanging out with friends, have caused immense pain and damage to their relationship. Understandably, Jill has made the difficult decision to leave him.

However, Jill's anger is further fueled when she learns that Dave has seemingly turned his life around. He has started working, bought a home for himself and his new wife, and even has children now. It's understandable that this new chapter in Dave's life has created a mix of emotions for Jill.

Whenever Jill wants to escape the haunting memories of the terrible things Dave has inflicted upon her, a malevolent demon stealthily creeps into her mind, replaying the vivid reel of torment she endured at his hands. As Jill navigates through the hardships of struggling to pay her bills, her heart weighs heavy with regret. She had sacrificed her cherished dreams on the altar of their ill-fated relationship, relinquishing her aspirations just to be by Dave's side. Yet now, as fate twists the knife deeper, she witnesses him thriving with someone else, the bitterness of resentment welling up within her soul.

The demon, a relentless phantom from her torment-ridden past, conjures images of each painful manipulation, every broken promise, and the shattered trust, Dave has either done or said to her. It fuels the fire of her righteous anger, fanning the flames of loathing in her heart. Despite her best efforts at moving forward, the sinister presence ensures that the agonizing memories remain etched in her consciousness. Jill must summon every ounce of strength to resist the alluring temptation to succumb to despair, for within her lies the power to forge a new path, reclaiming her dreams, and vanquishing the demon that threatens to consume her.

Years have passed by, and even though she's in a new relationship with a different man, her thoughts dwell upon the past because the same old demons refuse to allow her to have inner peace. And whenever she goes to church and talks with her pastor, he tells her, "You must learn to forgive him. Just let it go!" But isn't able to give her the necessary steps to properly forgive Dave.

Important Intel: **Matthew 18:21-35**, Yeshua informs us that its of necessity to forgive, because if we don't, then there will be serious consequences. Demons possess a keen awareness that residing within the human heart is a potent power - the act of forgiveness. They understand that when an individual fails to forgive from the depths of their being, they grant the demons permission to unleash their malevolent forces upon them. With wicked delight, these demons inflict torments and agonies upon their target, reveling in the pain they inflict.

Not content with mere physical afflictions, demons specialize in vexing their victims on a deeper, psychological level. They tirelessly work to make life harder than it should be, magnifying every challenge, every setback, and every dark emotion. Their goal is to impair one's mental well-being, driving them further away from solace and compassion.

Furthermore, demons possess the uncanny ability to connect their prey with individuals who add to their suffering. These malicious entities orchestrate encounters with those who amplify feelings of betrayal, resentment, and despair. These connections deepen the wounds of the spirit, intensifying the anguish experienced by their target.

So beware, for demons know that unforgiveness opens the gates to a relentless cycle of torment, pain, and despair. Only through true forgiveness can one break free from their clutches and find peace once more.

In conclusion: If a person doesn't forgive, neither will Yahweh forgive them, and if He doesn't forgive him or her, and if they die like this, and face the judgment, in the lake of fire shall they go! So, then the person needs to ask themselves this question, is it worth being tormented all the days of my life while on earth and afterward, die and be casted into the lake of fire, along with the Devil and his angels, or simply forgive and show the love of Jesus, and allow Him to avenge me.

Season One Attack Three: *Did You Hear About?*

Gossiping, a wicked weapon cunningly employed by demons, has wreaked havoc on the lives of billions throughout history. With every whisper, it ignites flames of destruction, engulfing families, friendships, and reputations. Its malevolent influence has caused irreparable damage, leading to broken bonds and shattered trust.

Within the confines of family units, gossiping acts as a corrosive force. It gnaws away at the foundation of love and unity, transforming once sacred connections into bitter battlegrounds. Secrets are exposed, confidences betrayed, and the tight-knit fabric of kinship unravels, leaving only heartache and sorrow.

Beyond the realms of blood ties, gossiping infiltrates friendships, leaving trails of alienation and sorrow in its wake. Thin threads of trust are severed, replaced by feelings of doubt and betrayal. Friends become foes as the power of malicious words takes hold, casting shadows of doubt on once cherished relationships.

Reputations, carefully built over time, can crumble under the weight of gossip's poisoned arrows. Innocence tarnished and character assassinated, victims find themselves unjustly judged and subject to scorn. The damage inflicted by this weapon of choice leaves scars that may never fully heal.

Gossiping's insidious influence goes even further, paving the way for ostracizing behavior and fostering forms of relational aggression. Individuals find themselves isolated, abandoned by those they thought they could rely on. They bear the burden of rumors and lies, prisoners of their own social exile.

In the hands of demons, gossiping is a formidable force, capable of tearing lives apart and leaving destruction in its wake. It is a warning to all of us to guard our tongues and resist the power of this insidious weapon.

Listen to what the bible says about the tongue: *"But the **tongue** can no man tame; it is **an unruly evil**, **full of deadly poison**. Therewith bless we God, even the Father; and therewith curse we men, which are made after* the similitude of God. Out of the **same mouth proceeds blessing and cursing**," James 3:8-10.

"And the **tongue is a fire**, a **world of iniquity**: so is the tongue among our members, that **it defiles the whole body**, and **set on fire the course of fire of hell**," James 3:6. The word iniquity means: injustice and wrong-doing.

In conclusion: the bible says that both death and life is in the words of a person [**Proverbs 18:21**], and therefore, a person can use their words to bring death, or life, destruction or rebuild, hatred or love, and so on. 99.99% of all gossipers are rapscallions.

Season One Attack Four: *Accuser Of The Brothern*

The dictionary defines the word "Accuser," as: to charge with a fault or offense: Blame. Or to bring an accusation.

In **Revelation 12:10,** the Bible reveals an important truth about Satan: he assumes the role of the accuser of the brethren. This means that he relentlessly tries to tempt us into doing wrong and immediately brings our misdeeds and words to the attention of God. Satan, in his cunning nature, hopes that by incessantly reporting every mistake we make, God will abandon us.

The passage highlights Satan's perpetual efforts to disrupt our fellowship with God. His never-ending accusations aim to create doubt, guilt, and separation between us and our Creator. Satan's ultimate desire is for us to falter and fall, believing that God will turn His back on us.

However, it is crucial to remember that while Satan may accuse us, God is a loving and compassionate Father. He sees beyond our flaws and is willing to forgive and restore us when we sincerely seek His forgiveness. Despite Satan's persistent accusations, God's grace prevails, providing us with hope, redemption, and the opportunity for a renewed relationship with Him.

In a world where pastors should be uniting in faith and spreading love and fighting against the works of the devil, it is disheartening to witness some tearing down their fellow shepherds, instead of being obedient to the word of God when He said, *"that if one of our brethren is overtaking in a fault, we should restore him* [**Galatians 6:1**]. We are not commission to do the Devil's job.

God, being aware of Satan's accusations, remains steadfast in His loyalty to His children and refuses to listen to the devil's claims when brought before Him. However, Satan, undeterred by this divine intervention, has resorted to inspiring others to participate in character destruction. The result: a painful reality where pastors are publicly exposing the faults of their colleagues, diminishing their standing in the eyes of the world. In all of my days, I have never seen a witch, psyche, medium, and such like, stand before their audience and publicly humiliate other witches, psyches, and mediums, like I have witness other ministers doing in these last days. These so-called pastors are more interested in calling out someone else's faults, than to exclaim the sins that are prevalent in many churches.

Alongside pastors, church members also bear the responsibility to care for one another. However, instead of embodying the love and support they are called to provide, some behave like the world, joining the movement of character destruction rather than being a source of comfort in times of fallen brothers and sisters. This departure from godly behavior not only perpetuates division but also erodes the core values that true believers stand for. It is crucial to remember that unity, compassion, and forgiveness are the principles that should guide our actions and strengthen our community.

In conclusion: How it must grieve the heart of our Heavily Father, when the very people, who asked for forgiveness when they did wrong, and don't want Yahweh to remember their evil deeds, but when another brother or sister in Christ falls, they feel the need to divulge it.

Season Two Attack One: *Grace As A License To Sin*

Because we're living under grace and mercy, not the law, many Christians are abusing the grace given to them by Jesus Christ. It is important to remember that sin is still destructive and teardown marriages, families, communities, and nations. Grace, however, doesn't empower a person to keep on sinning. In **Romans 6:1-2**, the Apostle Paul warns us that we should not continue in sin simply because we have received grace. Instead, grace enables us to die to our sinful nature.

While the law may enable a person to live under sin, grace empowers us to die to it. It is crucial to understand that all sins are wrong and must be punished accordingly. Grace should not be taken lightly or used as an excuse to continue engaging in sinful behavior. As Christians, it is our responsibility to strive for righteousness and actively resist the temptation to abuse the grace given to us.

Season Two Attack Two: *Spiritual Amnesia*

Spiritual Amnesia is a prevalent condition among Christians today. Despite regularly attending church services, many believers suffer from a disheartening lack of understanding regarding their true identity in Christ Jesus. They are oblivious to the immense power and authority bestowed upon them as children of Yahweh.

In a world where confusion over identity and gender prevails, it is crucial for us, as Christians, to retain absolute clarity about our position in Christ. While society grapples with questions of self, we must stand firmly rooted in the knowledge of who we are in Him.

Let us not succumb to the prevailing chaos and uncertainty. Instead, let our faith serve as an anchor in turbulent times. Embracing our identity as heirs of the Most-High, we can walk confidently, knowing that we possess the authority and power to overcome any challenge the world presents.

By studying God's Word, we can regain our spiritual memory, rediscovering the truth of our identity in Christ Jesus. As we reconnect with our divine heritage, let us radiate that truth to a world in dire need of hope and certainty.

I pray that in Yeshua's name, that today, right now, you fully regain your memory of who you are, as a child of Yahweh. Amen.

Season Two Attack Three: *I'll Do It Tomorrow*

Jesus warned us about the deceptions of Satan, who tempts people with the deadliest lie of all: "***You can do it tomorrow***." This deception preys on our tendency to procrastinate, pushing us to delay important actions and decisions. But Jesus reminded us to remain ready at all times, for life is fragile and unpredictable. One moment we may be alive, and the next we may be gone. We cannot take tomorrow for granted, as it is not promised to us.
The uncertainty of life should serve as a reminder to seize the opportunity that is right in front of us. Whatever it is that we can do now, we must do it

without hesitation. Death is coming for us all, marking the transition into eternal life or damnation. So let us not fall into Satan's trap of procrastination, but instead embrace the urgency of the present moment.

Season Two Attack Four: *Once Saved Always Saved*

While water baptism is a crucial step in one's spiritual journey, it should be understood that it alone does not guarantee access to heaven. This concept became evident to me during a conversation with a young man. Asking him if he was saved, he confidently responded that he had been baptized. I gently reassured him that while baptism is important, it is not sufficient for salvation. To truly secure one's eternal destiny, one must undergo a transformative experience of being born-again and commit to living a life in accordance with God's word.

It is true that water baptism symbolizes the washing away of sins and the beginning of a new life in Christ. However, it is the personal relationship with Jesus and obedience to His teachings that ultimately determine our salvation. Merely going through the act of baptism without genuine faith and a transformed heart does not ensure access to heaven.

So, my advice to the young man was clear: baptism is a crucial step, but it must be followed by a true conversion of heart, a genuine commitment to following after Christ Jesus, and living in accordance with God's word. It is this authentic connection with God that leads to salvation and prepares one for the eternal life with Him in heaven.

Season Three Attack One: *Free From Condemnation*

No more living under condemnation. For two decades, I had been living under condemnation. Going to church every time the doors opened, but because I wasn't taught the grace message, I lived under consistent attacks from the devil. In the past, when I sinned, I would beat myself up, and when I wasn't doing it, the devil took over, slandering me until I felt like the worst human being in the world. I experienced depression, feeling so ashamed and discouraged whenever I stumbled. It seemed like I was trapped in a never-ending cycle, falling to the same old sins time and again. It was a heavy burden to carry, and it kept me from experiencing true freedom and victory.

However, when I finally learned about grace, it was a game-changer. Understanding that God's love and forgiveness were not dependent on my ability to be perfect lifted the weight off my shoulders. I realized that I no longer had to condemn myself or let my past sins define me. With grace, I found the power to overcome my past sins, breaking free from the chains that held me captive for so long. Now, I walk in the light of God's love, confident that His grace is sufficient for me. No more condemnation, only freedom and victory.

Romans 8:1, *"Therefore, there is now no condemnation for those who are in Christ Jesus."* If a person falls, then he or she should ask Yahweh for forgiveness and then, turn away from that sin, by living under grace, not law!

Season Three Attack Two: *Overcoming Persecutions*

In **2nd Corinthians 4:8-11**, we are reminded of the challenges we might face as followers of Christ. Jesus tells us that if we are to reign with Him, we must also be prepared to suffer with Him. We may find ourselves troubled on every side, feeling perplexed and even persecuted, but in these moments, we must remember that we are not without hope.

Though we may face distress and despair, we are assured that we will not be overcome by them. Our faith in Jesus sustains us, and even in the face of adversities, we are not forsaken. When we feel cast down, we can find comfort in knowing that we will not be destroyed.

It is through these trials that we carry the dying of the Lord Jesus in our bodies, allowing His life to be made manifest in our mortal flesh. Just as Jesus overcame, so will we if we remain faithful to Him. In our suffering, we find strength, in our weaknesses, we find His power. Let us hold fast to our faith, knowing that through every challenge, victory awaits us.

Season Three Attack Three: *Spiritual Fatigue*

Spiritual fatigue is an all too familiar experience that affects us all at certain junctures in our journey. It is in these moments that we must remember that the adversary's prime objective is to exhaust the faithful, the saints of the Most-High God. Nevertheless, despite the weariness that attempts to take hold, we should not allow ourselves to succumb to despair. We must hold on to the understanding that our efforts in well doing will not be in vain.

It is precisely during these times of depletion that we must cling to the truth that in due season, a reward awaits us. If we can muster the strength to persevere and resist the impulse to give up, a fruitful outcome lies ahead. The Holy Spirit, the very essence of divine strength and comfort, encourages and uplifts us as we wage the spiritual battle. It is through His guidance and fortitude that we find the resolve to press forward, knowing that our labor is not in vain.

So, my fellow spiritual warriors, in the face of weariness and fatigue, let us take heart and find solace in the reminder that the battle is not ours alone. With the aid of the Holy Spirit, we shall prevail.

Season Three Attack Four: *Doubting Yahweh's Goodness*

In the battle against the character of God's goodness, Satan employs various tactics. One strategy is to instill doubt in individuals, causing them to question whether God truly possesses goodness. However, if doubts fail to arise within a person's heart, the devil will attempt a different approach. This time, Satan will subtly persuade the person that while God may indeed be good, He hasn't been good specifically to them.
This manipulative tactic aims to cast down their confidence in the goodness of God. It is a treacherous endeavor to convince individuals that God plays favoritism, showering blessings upon others but intentionally withholding them from the individual. Despite these relentless efforts, it is crucial for believers to cling to the truth that God is unwaveringly good, regardless of what circumstances may suggest.

Season Four Attack One: *Why Haven't God Provided For Me*

The devil cunningly targets believers with specific biblical passages to stir doubt within them. One verse he may weaponize is, "If you, being evil, know how to bless your children, how much more will your Father in heaven bless those who ask Him." By distorting this passage, the devil plants a seed of uncertainty, making believers doubt their identity as children of God.
Another verse he may exploit is, "It rains on the just and the unjust alike." Utilizing this scripture, the devil aims to make believers question why seemingly everyone except them receives God's blessings, even sinners. These devious tactics seek to deceive believers into believing that God is either incapable or unwilling to provide for their needs. However, it is crucial for believers to remain steadfast in their faith, trusting that God's love and care for them will prevail over the lies and doubts sown by the enemy.

Season Four Attack Two: *Why God Allow The Innocent To Suffer*

I heard an insightful physicist express his atheism, citing the occurrence of a devastating hurricane, that took the lives of serval hundreds of people, as evidence against God's existence. However, upon reflecting on his words, I recognized that his intelligence primarily resided in the realm of science, not in comprehending the nature of Yahweh.

It is true that bad things do happen to good people, but this does not imply that Yahweh lacks care or compassion. The ways and thoughts of God transcend human understanding, surpassing our finite comprehension. As stated in **Isaiah 55:8-9**, "For my thoughts are not your thoughts, neither are your ways my ways," declares the Lord. "As the heavens are higher than the earth, so are my ways higher than your ways and my thoughts than your thoughts."

Attempting to fully fathom God with our limited conscious minds is an exercise in futility. To do so would reduce the infinite nature of God to fit within the confines of our finite understanding. Therefore, it is humbling to acknowledge that we cannot truly grasp the entirety of God's being.

Season Four Attack Three: *Return Back To Previous Sins*

Every single day, while you and I are asleep, demons are gathering in the shadows, discussing and strategizing their cruel intentions. They are cunning creatures, ceaselessly plotting to entice us into returning to the clutches of our old sins. Their malevolent whispers resonate in the darkest corners of our minds, attempting to erode our faith and distance us from the splendid grace we once embraced.

In the words of the Bible: "For it is impossible, in the case of those who have once been enlightened, who have tasted the heavenly gift, and have shared in the Holy Spirit, and have tasted the goodness of the word of God and the powers of the age to come, and then have fallen away to restore them again to repentance, since they are crucifying once again the Son of God to their own harm and holding him up to contempt" (**Hebrews 6:4-6 ESV**).

Indeed, the notion that demons continually strive to allure us away from the light is a stark reminder of the endurance required to resist their temptations. Let us remain vigilant, constantly seeking the strength to withstand their insidious tactics and to stand firm in our commitment to righteousness.

Season Four Attack Four: *Feeling Rejected*

There are demons who are assigned to you, relentlessly attempting to convince you that God has rejected you. Their malicious job is to make you believe that your suffering is a direct result of God's abandonment. Moreover, these nefarious beings want nothing more than for you to accept the idea that nobody else loves or cares about you, leaving you with a hopeless desire to cease to exist.

However, it is crucial to remember that just because some individuals may have turned their backs on you, it does not mean that He will do the same to you. God questions, can a mother forget her child? It is indeed possible, but the all-knowing Lord insists that He will never leave nor forsake you. In the very palm of His hand, He has taken care to etch your name, signifying your deep significance and eternal connection to His unwavering love and support.

Season Addition Attack: *Confused About What Religion Is True*

There are sinister forces at work, using unsuspecting religious individuals as vessels to sow confusion and mislead those seeking the truth. These demons have assigned themselves the task of distorting the essence of religion, aiming to cloud your understanding of the one true path that leads to the divine.

Any religious belief that advocates for certain ideals should be viewed with suspicion, as they are tainted by demonic influence. Avoid doctrines that propagate the notion of gaining access to heaven through personal merits or good deeds. These teachings are deceptive and serve to steer you away from the true nature of salvation.

Beware of religions that promote the existence of multiple deities or endorse the idea that one can become their own god. Such ideas are rooted in the machinations of malevolent forces, seeking to divert you from the singular truth. Remember that there is only one route to heaven, as articulated by Jesus himself: "I am the way, the truth, and the life. No one can come to the Father except through me."

Remain vigilant and resolute in your quest for spirituality. Do not be swayed by the false promises and deceptive doctrines peddled by those under the influence of these demonic entities. Seek the truth, cling to it, and allow it to guide you towards the realm of the true and living God.

CASE EIGHT: Demons And Mental Illnesses

This may surprise you, but according to the bible, there were certain sickness and diseases, that are connected to demons. And when the devil or devils were cast out of the person, immediately, they received a miracle. So, then let's look at these scriptures.

1. There is an unclean spirit that holds the title of "spirit of infirmity," in **Luke 13:10-18**. Yeshua reference that this woman was a descendant of Abraham, but suffered from kyphosis for eighteen years, due to Satan's inflicting her. Her illness came from a devil.

2. In **Mark 9:17-27**, a man brought Yeshua his son, who had a "dumb spirit" within him, and asked Him could He cast it out. The dumb spirit caused the young boy to:

- Cut himself   • To foam at the mouth   • Bit down on his teeth
- pine away   • Attempted suicide

3. "**Matthew 8:16**," the bible says that many people came to Yeshua, and when He casted the devil out of them, and all that were sick, were healed. You must understand that sicknesses and disease didn't come from Yahweh, but rather from the devil.

4. In **Matthew 12:22**, that when the devil was casted out of the people, those who couldn't speak and the blind were healed. This verse shows that a demon prohibited some of them from speaking and being able to see physically.

5. In "**Acts 8:7**," when unclean spirits were casted out, many of them who were paralyzed were healed.

Please here me, if a person is currently suffering from any of these things, this doesn't necessary means that they are possessed with a devil, but rather that a demon is behind these kinds of sickness and diseases. I personally believe that ever kind of mental illness are caused by demons.

Let's look at "**Matthew 10:1**," *And when He had called unto Him His twelve disciples, He gave them power against unclean spirits, to cast them out, and to heal all manner of sickness and all manner of disease.*
Special Comment: As a disciple of Yeshua, you or no one around you have the right to have an unclean spirit within them, to be sick, and or, to have a disease, when He has giving you the power and authority to bring deliverance to them.

"And ought not his woman, a daughter of Abraham whom Satan bound for eighteen years, be loosed from this bond on the Sabbath day?" (**Luke 13:16**). More than likely, this woman had what is known as "Kyphosis," also referred to as "bent spine syndrome." This woman condition was caused by Satan.

There's no mental illness, sickness, disease, that is stronger than the name of Yeshua. The problem doesn't lie in Jesus' name, but rather in this, "Are you really His disciple, because He cannot lie?"

CASE NINE *Know Thou Enemies:*

After studying this chapter, you should be able to:

- understand battle plans
- understand the different forms of lust
- know who is your enemy
- where is your enemy
- know your enemy capabilities
- the difference between haters versus enemies

Victory or defeat begins in the mind, not when a person picks up a weapon and enters the battle field. And this stands true for every battle fought, whether on the physical battlefield or spiritual one. The outcome of any endeavor is often predetermined long before the first step is taken or the first blow is struck. It is the thoughts and beliefs that shape a person's mindset that determine their success or failure.

A battle is not solely fought by the might of physical weapons or the strength of armies. It is fought first and foremost within one's own mind and in the spiritual world. The battlefield of the mind is where beliefs are forged, where confidence is built, and where determination is tested. The person who enters the battlefield with a clear vision of victory, with unwavering faith in their faith in Yahweh, has already won half the battle, the other half is when they show up.

Conversely, the one who succumbs to doubts and fears, who harbors thoughts of defeat, and indecision, is already defeated before taking up a firearm or, trying to use the sword of the spirit to do battle. Long before a shot is fired, the victory or defeat was decided. It is the mental resilience and fortitude that pave the way for triumph or tragedy. So, if one wishes to emerge victorious in any battle, they must cultivate a mindset of Christ Jesus, for it is written, "Let this mind be in you, which was also in Christ Jesus.

In the relentless struggle between good and evil, the mind stands as an epic battleground. At the forefront of this spiritual warfare, Satan lurks, seeking to plant seeds of doubt, fear, confusion, shame, hate, regrets, and lies within the deepest recesses of a person's thoughts. With cunning precision, he attacks relentlessly, preying upon those who aren't wearing the helmet of salvation, exploiting every crack and crevice in the mind's defenses. Armed with deception and temptation, he cunningly manipulates the vulnerable, twisting perceptions and distorting reality.

The mind, a magnificent citadel of thoughts and emotions, becomes the focal point of this relentless assault. Satan's dark whispers infiltrate like poison, sowing seeds of negativity, self-doubt, and despair.
He capitalizes on weaknesses, exploiting fears and insecurities to dismantle the very foundation of one's peace and sanity. It is within the fog of this internal battle that one must stand strong, armed with faith, resilience, and a steadfast belief in one's own worth. Only by recognizing the mind as a battlefield can one hope to repel the insidious attacks, triumphing over darkness with the guiding light of truth.

Every second, minute, hour in the day, every week, in the month, throughout the year, devils are trying to gain access into a person's mind; they're not satisfied with being a part of an individual's life, no, they are passionate about governing over the person's entire life. But, let's go deeper into what Satan's battle plans so we may better prepare ourselves in these last days.
Satan have three main battle plans, in order to bring about the destruction of all humans, which are these:

1. The lust of the flesh   2. The lust of the eyes   3. The pride of life

"For all that is in the world, the lust of the flesh, the lust of the eyes, and the pride of life, is not of the Father but is of the world," **1st John 2:16**.

The Lust of the Flesh: The lust of the flesh, though enticing and alluring, carries with it a myriad of dangers that can consume one's life if left unchecked. It is a primal desire that blinds reason and tempts individuals to indulge in pleasures that bring temporary gratification, but destroys their relationship with Yeshua, hindering spiritual fruits and disrupting their spiritual gifts. For Moses chose to suffer the afflictions with the people of Yahweh, then to enjoy the pleasures of sin for a season, **Hebrews 11:25**.

One of the greatest dangers of succumbing to the lust of the flesh is the erosion of self-control. When driven purely by physical desires, individuals lose their ability to make rational decisions, often falling into a vicious cycle of addiction and self-destruction, and eventually, living the remaining of their days, miserable and regretful. Moreover, the lust of the flesh can also lead to the deterioration of important relationships. The insatiable appetites that accompany this lust can cause individuals to betray the trust of their loved ones, damaging bonds that may take a lifetime to repair.

Furthermore, the dangers extend beyond the personal realm. Society as a whole suffers when the lust of the flesh becomes normalized and prioritized above all else. It distorts values, promotes unhealthy behaviors, and can contribute to the breakdown of communal harmony.

In light of these dangers, it is crucial to walk daily in the Holy Spirit [**Galatian 5:16**], in order to avoid fulfilling one own's fleshly desires. Only through submitting completely to Yahweh and crucifying our flesh daily, can individuals strive towards a balanced and fulfilling life.

Demons uses the individual's own lustful desires to wedge war against them, for what better and easier way to destroy a person, then to use what they're already craving for. No offense, but it's like an obese man who has very high blood pressure, no pills to lower it, and yet, pleading with his enemy to give him the five porkchops that his enemy purposely purchased, just for the obese person demise, so he can eat all of them for his dinner. Demons know that all sins, whether a person view some of them as more lethal than others, are all designed to destroy people's lives.

The Lust of the Eyes: The dangers of the lust of the eyes are manifold, permeating various aspects of our lives. Succumbing to this insidious temptation will lead to disastrous consequences, both for ourselves and anyone who's connected to us.

First, the lust of the eyes often blinds us to our true priorities and our responsibilities. It lures us with its glimmering facade, distracting us from what truly matters in life and therefore, focus on superficial things. Our relentless pursuit of material possessions and temporal pleasures consumes us, leaving us empty, unfulfilled, and full of regrets.

Moreover, this insatiable desire corrupts our judgment and distorts our perception of reality, causing a person to embrace fraudulent things, rather than things that healthy for us. It clouds our ability to make rational decisions, leading us down treacherous paths filled with immoral actions and reckless behavior. From impulsive spending sprees to illicit affairs, the lust of the eyes can steer us towards moral bankruptcy.

Furthermore, the lust of the eyes fosters a culture of comparison and envy. Constantly comparing ourselves to others breeds discontentment, eroding our self-esteem and fostering resentment towards those who possess what we desire. This toxic cycle perpetuates a society marked by unhealthy competition and fractured relationships.

In essence, the dangers of the lust of the eyes lie in its ability to warp our values, blind our judgment, and sow seeds of discontentment. To resist its allure, we must cultivate inner contentment, focus on meaningful connections, and prioritize our true well-being above material pursuits.

The Pride of Life: The pride of life, although captivating, carries along with it a string of dangers that can ensnare even the most resilient souls. It is a seductive force that entices individuals to seek validation, influence, and superiority over others. In the pursuit of material possessions, social status, or personal achievements, one often falls prey to its treacherous grip, blinding them to the true essence of life.

First and foremost, the dangers of the pride of life lie in its ability to breed arrogance and ego. When consumed by this insatiable desire for recognition, individuals lose touch with their authentic selves, neglecting empathy and compassion. Relationships suffer as selfishness takes precedence over genuine connection, leading to isolation and loneliness.

Moreover, the pride of life can create a perpetual cycle of discontentment. One is never satisfied with their accomplishments, always striving for more accolades, possessions, or power. This constant hunger for validation fuels a scarcity mindset, overshadowing gratitude and the joys of simplicity.

As we navigate through life, it is essential to recognize these dangers and seek a balance between ambition and humility. Embracing a mindset rooted in kindness, gratitude, and genuine connections can shield us from the allure of the pride of life, allowing us to find true fulfillment and meaning.
I am astonished at the number of Christians who are totally oblivious to Satan's tricks, and yet, when they're attacked by demons and suffer great lost, they're surprised at being defeated. For years in church, I was taught about the things of Yahweh, but very little about the demons. In fact, I was taught that they're all evil, tell lies, and want all humans to die and go to hell; and while this is true, there is much more to them than this.

Beginning Of My Ministry: When I first started street ministry, I was a novice in regards to how demons operate and their powers over certain communities and regions, but because I was invited by an older brother in the Lord God to help and assist him, I decided to evangelize the word of God with him.
We went to an area where prostitution, drugs, and alcohol were prevalent. And though I wasn't tempted to engage in any of these things, I was in my early stage of being delivered from fornication.

During our interaction with people, I felt very uncomfortable, not because of the sinner's behaviors, but rather the message from the older brother in the Lord God, who consistently used destructive criticism like: *"You all need to come to God right now, are else you'll going to hell."*

The Bible informs us to be wise as a serpent and yet, harmless as a dove. Yes, if they didn't repent, they were going to hell, but the correct way would have been if he had said, *"Listen, God loves you and He sent His Son Jesus Christ to die for your sins, so you don't have to live in them and one day, perish in hell, but rather to live with Him in heaven when you leave this world."* This isn't to say that they would have repented at a softer tone, but rather we are commissioned to show love as well.

Every time we when out to evangelize, he continued with his destructive criticism, so I decided to relinquish from him and street ministry. We weren't causing anyone to repent and shortly afterward, I started getting attacked with lustful thoughts, and other strong attacks from demonic powers.
The older brother's wife, begin attacking him, she started mimicking signs of demonic behavior within the church and sowing discord among the

saints, and had to be expelled from it, and shortly afterward, the older brother mysteriously died.

I didn't say any of this to cause you to become fearful, but rather informed. When you decide to fight against the kingdom of darkness, demons are going to attack back.

Important Information: Demons know all of your weaknesses, and when you attempt to attack them, they're going to either tempt you with your weakness or, have someone else to attack you, in order to stop your mission, so be ready!

Battle Plans One: I strongly recommend that if you're going to evangelize in a certain region:
- first, don't be a novice, beyond having a strong relationship with Yeshua, also become educated about demons and how to effectively fight with them
- second, know what kind of demonic forces you will be encountering. By understand the problems or crimes occurring within that community, will help you to know what you're about to encounter.
- third, be both wise as a serpent, while harmless as a dove.
- Have your house in order, because as are attacking their wicked kingdom, they are going to attack your home.

Let's read about what the Bible says and suggest about going to war:
"*Or what king, going out to encounter another king in war, will not sit down first and deliberate whether he is able with ten thousand to meet him who comes against him with twenty thousand? And if not, while the other is yet a great way off, he sends a delegation and asks for terms of peace,*" **Luke 14:31-32 ESV**.

Jesus was revealing that a wise king will first think about or discuss issues and decision carefully before going to war, because he cannot afford to be impetuous, unless he desires to lose many soldiers, land, position, and his standing with others. So, then, if he's unable to win against his enemy, before going to war, he will send an ambassador and make peace.

General Plans:

Understanding battle plans is crucial for a general as it serves as the foundation for victory on the battlefield. Here are a few reasons why it is important for a general to understand battle plans:

Strategic Advantage: Battle plans provide a strategic advantage by outlining the objectives, resources, and timeline of a military campaign. A general who comprehends these plans can make informed decisions, exploit weaknesses, and seize opportunities.

In the Spirit: We as Christians are considered as soldiers for our Lord God [**Ephesians 6:10-18**], and therefore, we are commanded to put on the entire armor of Yahweh, in order to withstand and overcome the schemes of the devil. The whole armor of the Lord gives us the advantage on the battlefield against demons.

Besides accepting salvation, putting on the entire armor of Yahweh is His second plan for humanity and the first line of defense, but not only against demonic forces, also against one's own negative thoughts and protection from their haters and enemies.

Coordination and Communication: Battle plans enable effective coordination and communication among troops and commanders. Understanding the plan allows the general to convey precise orders, ensuring that all units work together seamlessly to achieve the desired outcome.

In the Spirit: The Holy Spirit is our general, and he communicates with us through His word [**Matthew 4:4**], dreams [**Joe/Job 33:14-15**] His holy servants [**Matthew 10:40**], by giving us a heart to know and understand Him [**Jeremiah 31:33**], and speaking to us. Therefore, when we listen to His instructions, we win! In addition, He will connect us to other believers, so we can work in cohesion and defeat our enemies [**Deuteronomy 32:30**].

Adaptability: Effective battle plans include contingencies for various scenarios. A knowledgeable general can adapt the plan to changing battlefield conditions, making necessary adjustments and exploiting unforeseen opportunities in real-time.

In the Spirit: As a child of Yahweh, it is of necessity for a believer to be able to move with the Holy Spirit, without wavering. Furthermore, a Chirstian must be able to adopt to our modern times, but not conforming to its image.

Resource Allocation: Battle plans include resource allocation strategies, such as manpower, ammunition, and infrastructure. A general who understands these plans can efficiently allocate resources, maximizing the military's capabilities while minimizing wastage.

Risk Mitigation: Battle plans involve risk analysis and mitigation strategies. By comprehending the plans, a general can anticipate potential risks, plan for alternative courses of action, and minimize the impact of unforeseen challenges.

In conclusion, understanding battle plans empowers the general to make informed decisions, effectively communicate with troops, adapt to changing circumstances, allocate resources efficiently, and reduce risks. It is vital for a general to master battle plans to achieve victory on the battlefield.

Exercise: What battle plans do you have for you and your family?

Special Comment: Never prepare for war when on the battlefield, no, prepare for it during peaceful times! So many Christians in today's world, wait until they're being spiritual attacked, then they want to take up arms, but it's too late then. Therefore, write up a battle plan for yourself and family. How have demons previously attacked you and your family? How are you planning to counteract their attacks and to defeat them this time?

Every General must know these three critical things:

- Who is my enemy
- Where is my enemy
- What is my enemy capabilities

Without knowing these three valuable things, it would be nothing short of a suicidal mission to fight against one's adversary.

Who Is My Enemy: Understanding who's your enemy, truly holds immense significance as it allows you to safeguard your interests, protect yourself, and navigate through challenging situations with clarity and vigilance. Acquiring knowledge about your enemy is crucial as it unveils their intentions, motivations, and potential threats they pose to you.

By unveiling the identity of your enemy, you can be better prepared to counter their actions, defenses, and methods. Understanding their objectives and underlying reasons helps you anticipate their moves, strategize accordingly, and potentially outsmart them.

Moreover, identifying your enemy helps to distinguish between allies and adversaries, ensuring that you don't unknowingly trust or collaborate with individuals or entities that could harm you or jeopardize your mission. It enhances your decision-making skills, enabling you to align yourself with those who share the same values and goals as you.

Ultimately, knowing who your enemy is empowers you to protect your interests, maintain your safety, and navigate the complexities of life with heightened awareness and discernment. It is through this understanding that you can effectively defend yourself and pursue your aspirations unimpeded.

Important Intel: While many people mistakenly believe that haters and enemies are the same, the reality is that they are quite different. Haters are individuals who simply do not like you; they may speak negatively about you, criticize your abilities and work, and try to avoid your presence whenever possible. When forced to interact with you, their conversations are usually short and devoid of genuine interest.

Furthermore, haters will do their utmost to persuade others to share their negative opinions.
On the other hand, an enemy goes beyond these actions. They actively seek to connect with individuals who can bring harm to you. Enemies will approach you with friendship, gaining your trust and learning your secrets. They consistently ask you questions, extracting information to use against you while carefully avoiding any personal revelations.

Moreover, enemies will ask cunning questions in front of those who can harm you, waiting for you to slip up. Despite appearing helpful, their true aim is to dismantle your achievements and sabotage your work behind the scenes.

Therefore, it becomes evident that haters and enemies possess distinct characteristics and motivations, distinguishing them in their treatment of others.

Where Is My Enemy: Knowing the enemy's location is vital for several reasons. First, it allows for strategic planning and tactical maneuvers. By knowing the enemy's whereabouts, you can devise effective strategies to counter their movements and gain the upper hand in battle. It enables you to position your forces in advantageous positions and launch surprise attacks, diminishing their ability to defend themselves.

Secondly, awareness of the enemy's location enhances situational awareness. It helps identify potential threats and vulnerabilities, minimizing the risks for your own troops or assets. Additionally, knowing where the enemy is concentrated can provide insights into their intentions, allowing you to preempt their actions and stay one step ahead.

Moreover, knowledge of the enemy's location facilitates the coordination of resources. It allows you to allocate forces and assets appropriately to the areas that need defense or support, optimizing your overall operational efficiency.

Overall, understanding the enemy's location is crucial as it enhances strategic decision-making, situational awareness, and coordination, ultimately increasing the likelihood of a successful outcome in any conflict or competition.

Exercise: Do you know where is your enemy? What area in your life is the devil most likely to attack you in? How prepared are you if and when he attacks you in that particular area?

What Is My Enemy's Capabilities: Knowing your enemy's capabilities is crucial for several reasons. First, it allows you to assess the level of threat or danger they pose. Understanding what your enemy is capable of helps you gauge their strengths and weaknesses, enabling you to develop effective strategies to counter or mitigate their actions.

Secondly, knowledge of your enemy's capabilities helps you anticipate and prepare for potential attacks or actions. By knowing their resources, skills, and potential tactics, you can better anticipate their moves and develop proactive defense mechanisms.

Thirdly, understanding your enemy's capabilities provides insight into their motivations and intentions. It allows you to decipher their objectives, agendas, and potential vulnerabilities, which can be leveraged to neutralize their effectiveness.

Furthermore, knowledge of your enemy's capabilities enhances decision-making in conflict situations. It allows you to assess the risks involved, evaluate potential consequences, and choose the most suitable course of action.

In summary, understanding your enemy's capabilities is vital for assessing threats, foreseeing possible moves, uncovering vulnerabilities, and making informed decisions. It is an essential ingredient in any successful defensive or offensive strategy.

<u>Demons Hatred For Yahweh and His Saints:</u> On a scale from 1 to 5, where five represents the highest intensity, the most extreme god-hater would rank at a level 2, resembling a level 2 tornado. In stark contrast, all demons' hatred for God and his saints would be at a level 5, akin to facing a level 5 tornado. The depth of demons' hatred surpasses human comprehension, making it almost unfathomable. Just as a level 5 tornado unleashes unparalleled destruction, demons' animosity towards God and his followers is on a level that far exceeds any human capacity to understand.

Without rest, demons relentlessly cast aspersions, uttering blasphemous and incendiary remarks towards the Almighty God and his saints. To find respite, these malicious entities must fulfill three conditions: firstly, inhabiting a person's heart or mind; secondly, prompting that individual to unleash Satan's dominion upon the world; and lastly, daily defaming Yahweh and his faithful followers. Until these tasks are completed, the demons know no peace, forever tormenting and sowing discord in their relentless pursuit of chaos and corruption.

In the spirit, I witnessed the unsettling sight of demons expressing their intense hatred towards God. Their words and gestures were filled with a level of distain that is beyond comprehension. It was terrifying to see how their contempt for Yahweh surpassed that of the most notorious god-haters in history. Day and night, their mouths spewed forth violence, malice, death, and deceit, painting a chilling portrait of their malevolent nature. The intensity of their animosity towards God was palpable, leaving no doubt about the depths of their wickedness and rebellion.

While the demons were talking among themselves, each one expressed their strongest hatred for Yahweh and his saints. Each evil spirit tried to outdo the previous one who spoke, expressing unimaginable hatred. Then they made blasphemous words and perverted gestures toward God, so offensive that I have decided not to write it. The darkness of their malice and the intensity of their animosity were truly disturbing, sending a chill down the spine of even the most hardened souls. It was a sight and sound that one could not easily forget, a stark reminder of the eternal battle between good and evil.

The most shocking thing is, that demons believe that God is the guilty one, they are innocent of all charges. They believe that it was God who had sinned, not them. They believe that all of their actions and behaviors were justifiable and rational, and that God is a bully.

CASE TEN: **Doctrine Of Demons For These Last Days**:

The Bible has revealed that demons actually have a doctrine they're teaching within these last days, but what is this insidious indoctrinate?

[1] "Now the Spirit speaks expressly, that in the latter times some shall *depart from the faith*, giving heed to *seducing spirits*, and doctrines of devils; [2] *Speaking lies in hypocrisy*; having *their conscience seared with a hot iron*; [3] *Forbidding to marry*, and *commanding to abstain from meats*, which God has created to be received with thanksgiving of them which believe and know the truth," **1st Timothy 4:1-3**. So, then let's understand these six malignant teachings from these evil entities.

First False Doctrine *Departing From The Faith*:

The bible says: "*But without faith, it is impossible to please him [God], for he that comes to God must believe that he is, and that he is a rewarder of them that diligently seek him,*" **Hebrews 11:6**.

So, then it is the plan of demons is to separate believers and people from believing, trusting, and obeying Yahweh. In this modern day, you have motivated coaches teaching their listeners and followers how to put their faith in the universe, rather than in the one who created it.

Demons know that if they can shake the person from their faith in Yahweh, he or she will immediately start pleasing themselves, or other people.

The average church goer doesn't even bring their bible to church anymore, but rather has downloaded it to their cell phone. But you may ask, "What's wrong with reading your bible from your phone?"

The bible says, "*Study to show yourself approved unto God, a workman that needs not to be ashamed, rightly dividing the word of truth,*" **2nd Timothy 2:15**.

It is unlikely for a person to **study the bible** when they have downloaded it on their cell phone; and while it isn't impossible for them to do so, the probability of them doing so is improbable.

Once demons have shaken the person's faith in Yahweh, that individual will stop coming to Him, and as a result, will begin seeking other alternatives and resources, that doesn't contain God. He or she will search for other things to reward them, instead of the Lord God. And finally, they will seek after materialistic things and relationships, but godly things will no longer be relevant for them.

Second False Doctrine: Seducing Spirits

Beware the perilous allure of an enticing evil spirit, for its cunning lies in its ability to captivate and beguile. Like a seductive dance, it lures its victims into a web of deceit and manipulation, clouding their judgment and corrupting their souls. This malevolent entity feeds upon the vulnerability of the unsuspecting, weaving an intricate tapestry of illusions and whispers that ensnare its prey.

Its enticing spirit is intoxicating, drawing you closer with promises of power, pleasure, or fulfillment, only to strip you of your essence. Once entangled, escape becomes an arduous task, for this nefarious presence thrives on your fear and weakness. Nightmares become your reality; dreams tainted by its venomous touch.

Vigilance is your armor, shielding against this tempting specter. Do not underestimate the danger it poses; for its enticing spirit masks an insidious force, yearning to consume those who dare to succumb.

Q. Why is a seducing spirit so strong?

A. Because they tempt the person with their own evil desires or weakness; by surrounding the person around the things that he or she likes or love, but it is harmful for them. For instance, if a man has health problems and has a sweet-teeth [craving sweets], but his doctor has informed him that he must reframe from eating such foods.

Then, it is the duty of a demon is to put such foods around this man's environment. While driving to the grocery store, to make sure his eyes catch a bulletin board that has some kind of dessert that he loves, while in the grocery store, the demon will make sure he has to pass by the sweet section, while in the checkout line, show him snacks in the shopping cart of the person standing directly in front of him or right beside the check out.

Third False Doctrine: *Lies In Hypocrisy*

Lies in hypocrisy refer to the deceptive actions or statements carried out by individuals who pretend to be morally upright or follow a particular set of values while engaging in dishonest or contradictory behavior. It is when someone portrays themselves as virtuous, honest, or ethical, but their actions prove otherwise.

These lies in hypocrisy can take various forms, such as a politician advocating for transparency while engaging in corrupt practices behind closed doors or a preacher preaching about compassion while harboring hatred in their heart.

The essence lies in the contradiction between what is professed and what is actually practiced. It is a betrayal of trust and a distortion of one's true character. Ultimately, lies in hypocrisy can erode credibility, damage relationships, and hinder genuine progress or change.

Therefore, it is the doctrine of demons that blinds the individual from seeing that they are actually a hypocrite, destructive criticism or condemning others while secretly, they themselves are doing far worse than the person or people they are accusing.

The Fourth False Doctrine: *Seared Conscience*

A seared conscience refers to a state of moral apathy or emotional callousness towards one's actions or decisions. It suggests a condition where an individual's sense of right and wrong becomes desensitized or dulled, leading to a diminished ability to feel guilt or remorse for their behavior.

A seared conscience can arise from repetitive engagement in unethical or morally questionable actions, gradually numbing the individual's moral compass. It often manifests as an indifference to the consequences of their actions, an inability to empathize with others, or a disregard for ethical boundaries.

Those with a seared conscience may exhibit a lack of remorse, rationalize their behavior, or even engage in unethical conduct without experiencing any internal conflict. It is a concerning state of mind that can have adverse effects on personal relationships, professional ethics, and overall societal well-being.

Recognizing and addressing a seared conscience requires self-reflection, introspection, and a willingness to confront one's own values and beliefs. It involves re-establishing a connection with one's moral compass to restore empathy, accountability, and integrity in one's choices and actions.

The Fifth False Doctrine: Forbidden To Marry

The fifth doctrine of demons is to prevent the marriage between a man and woman. One day, while at work, I was talking with two young men and they asked me was I married, and which I happily said, "Yes!"

Their next word was somewhat surprising when they said, "But why?" And before I could answer, the other one said, "There is no real benefit to be married to someone, because the system is designed for the woman to receive everything if you'll divorce; even if she's the one who commit the infidelity."

They went on to say, "the judge is going to give her the house if you'll have one, the car, the children, and you will have to pay a large sum of child-support and alimony, she's entitled to your benefits if you retire and so on." So, why get married?

Instantaneously, I realized that these young men had been indoctrinated with the doctrine of demons, and there was nothing that I could tell them that was going to change their minds. Misogynistic words filled their mouths, as they released incendiary words toward women, including against their own mothers.

Why we need the Holy Ghost? While they were speaking misogyny words, the Holy Spirit through me, counteracted their inflammatory words by saying this, *"there is a difference between a woman and a lady. Whenever a girl reaches a certain age, depending upon her country, is considered a woman automatically when she arrives at that age, but that doesn't make her a lady. Just like when a boy reaches a certain age, he isn't considered as a boy any longer, but just because his age has made him a legal adult, doesn't make him a gentleman."*

You don't get the kind of woman you want, but rather the one you are; in other words, if you're not a gentleman, then you're not able to draw a lady into your life and vise versal.

If a man is perverted, then he's going to draw a promiscuous woman into his life. An honest man will draw a noble woman into his life. A dishonest man will not become romantically involved with a dishonest woman and vise-versal.

When the Holy Spirit spoke these words out of my mouth, they were astonished and became silent.

The bible says, *"He that finds a wife, has obtain favor from the Lord,"* but that's why we need to study the bible, instead of just reading it, so we can rightly divide the word of truth. It is asinine for a man to think just because he has married some woman, that he has obtained favor from God, even if she attends church regularly. While she might be a good woman, doesn't necessary mean that she is a good fit for him.

I have heard women who are 'only fans' workers, say that they are good women, and really believe it. Every woman who considers themselves a feminist, all believe and think that they're good and strong women. But just because a person believes themselves to be a good and moral person, doesn't make them such.

95% of the men and women I have talked with over the years, all viewed themselves are good individuals, in spite of their many shenanigans.

The Bible says, *"It is better to marry, then to burn in hell of fire,"* **1st Corinthians 7:9**. Therefore, if a couple [man and woman] are in a sexual relationship, and one of them die without being married to each other, according to the bible, he or she is going to hell of fire; which is the ultimate plan of the devil for every human.

The Sixth False Doctrine: Avoiding Eating Meats

While it's a person choice whether they will become a vegan or not, it's wrong when that individual tries to impose and force their beliefs upon others. Everyone must choose for themselves, what is better for him or her.

Satan's Ultimate Plan: *Stop The Gospel*

Matt. 24 [14] "*And this gospel of the kingdom shall be preached in all the world for a witness unto all nations; and then shall the end come.*"

In the ongoing spiritual battle, the devil is ceaselessly striving to hinder the widespread reach of the gospel. It is Satan's malicious ambition to thwart the message of hope, redemption, and salvation that the gospel brings to mankind. Understanding the transformative power of the gospel, Satan recognizes the threat it poses to his kingdom of darkness.

He employs various strategies to obstruct its progress, sowing seeds of doubt, confusion, and persecution in the hearts of individuals and societies. By sowing discord among believers, causing cultural divisions, and manipulating ideologies, Satan tries to extinguish the flame of the gospel's truth.

He subtly influences minds, aiming to distort the message and undermine its credibility. Yet, in the face of this relentless opposition, the gospel persists, shining its light into the darkest corners of the world, reminding us of the power and unwavering nature of God's love.

The gospel is the only source of power and authority that can heal the broken-hearted, proclaim liberty to the captivities, to open the prison doors to those bound by the devil, to comfort those who are mourning, restoring those who have suffered lost, giving them beauty for ashes, true joy in exchange for their sadness, and to uproot the evils in this world.

Did you know that the bible is illegal and or severely persecuted in 52 countries?

1. Afghanistan
2. Iran
3. Kazakhstan
4. Kyrgyzstan
5. Maldives
6. Mauritania
7. North Korea
8. Saudi Arabia
9. Somalia
10. Tajikistan
11. Turkmenistan
12. Uzbekistan
13. Yemen
14. Algeria
15. Bhutan
16. Brunei
17. China
18. Cuba
19. Djibouti
20. Eritrea
21. Kuwait
22. Laos
23. Libya
24. Malaysia
25. Morocco
26. Oman

27. Sudan	28. Tunisia
29. Bahrain	30. Bangladesh
31. Columbia	32. Egypt
33. Center African	34. Ethiopia
35. India Republic	36. Iraq
37. Jordan	38. Kenya
39. Lebanon	40. Mali
41. Myanmar Burma	42. Nepal
43. Niger	44. Nigeria
45. Pakistan	46. Philippine
47. Sri Lanka	48. Syria Mindanao
49. Tanzania	50. Turkey
51. United Arab Emirates	52. Vietnam

Special Comment: No matter how Satan and his demons try to stop the spread of the gospel, is totally futile. It would be easier and more believable for a man to stand in the pathway of a F-5 tornado and to knock it off its course, than for him to stop the move of Yahweh.

Satan and his demons are hoping that by attempting to slow down the spread of the gospel, it will delay Yeshua second return. After Yeshua second return [rapture has taken place], and the Israelites make a covenant with the beast [_antichrist_] he and his demons will only have seven years left, before they spend eternity in the Lake of Fire.

CASE ELEVEN   *Satan's Plans*

Here's a list of 30 common plans of Satan to bring about destruction for all humanity. These plans serve as the foundation for Satan's schemes to sow confusion, create divisions, inflict pain, ignite wars, and ultimately bring death. In the future, I intend to expand on these 30 plans and compile a comprehensive list of 66 sinister strategies employed by Satan to orchestrate humanity's downfall in my upcoming book titled "The 66 Plans of Satan's Sinister Agenda: Unveiling the Blueprint for Humanity's Demise." Stay tuned for a deeper exploration of how these diabolical plans aim to undermine the very fabric of human existence.

Satan's First Plan: *Focusing Upon Your Storm*

Satan's plan one is cunningly devised: to divert your attention towards the tempest that engulfs you, rather than fixating on the one who possesses the power to rescue you from its clutches. A vivid illustration of this scheme unfolded when Peter embarked upon the impossible, stepping onto the tumultuous surface of the water. As long as his gaze remained fixed upon the face of Jesus, his steps remained steady and firm.

He defied the natural order and walked upon the very substance that would've swallowed him whole. But alas, the sonorous roar of the mighty waves encroached upon Peter's hearing, and doubts began to assail his mind. He questioned the audacity of walking on water, and gradually, he succumbed to the sinking depths. If only Peter had retained his focus on the one who had beckoned him forth, Jesus, instead of being daunted by his arduous surroundings, he might have triumphed over his momentary affliction.

Beware, for this is Satan's plot: to shift your attention from the omnipotent Savior, thus paving the way for your demise. Stay steadfast, never lose sight of the one who can deliver you from any storm.

Satan's Second Plan: *Exalt Your Knowledge Over Yahweh*

Satan's devious second plan revolves around tempting individuals to exalt their own knowledge above that of Yahweh's. It entails instigating people to rely primarily on their own understanding, rather than acknowledging the wisdom and guidance of the Lord God. However, it is crucial for us to heed the counsel: "Rely not upon your own understanding, but in all your ways, acknowledge the Lord and he shall direct your paths." This fundamental principle emphasizes the importance of placing our trust in God's omniscience and seeking His guidance rather than solely relying on our limited human comprehension.

Yahweh has equipped us with a powerful spiritual weapon, capable of demolishing every high thought or idea that positions itself against His divine understanding. By embracing this weapon, we are enabled to cast down any concept or ideology that exalts itself above God's wisdom. Consequently, we are invited to humbly submit our thoughts and reasoning to the Lord, allowing His infinite knowledge to illuminate our path and guide us towards righteousness and truth.

Satan's Third Plan: *Speak Against God's Perfect Plan*

Satan's third plan centers around his desire for us to prioritize saying things that are acceptable or pleasing to other people, even when they contradict the teachings of Yahweh. This scheme was especially evident when Jesus spoke of his forthcoming sufferings and sacrifice for the sins of the world. At that moment, Peter's emotions overpowered him, offering an opportunity for Satan to speak through his mouth. Consequently, Peter rebuked what Jesus had said. Jesus, fully aware of Satan's influence in that moment, swiftly responded, "Get out of my face, Satan! You utter the things that appease humanity, but hold no favor with God."

This incident serves as a poignant reminder of Satan's cunning ploy to sway us towards seeking approval from others rather than aligning our thoughts and words with the divine truths. It serves to teach us the importance of discernment, where we must strive to prioritize the will of God over pleasing mankind, recognizing that speaking in line with Yahweh's teachings is paramount, even if it contradicts popular opinion.

Satan's Fourth Plan: *Spiritual Amnesia*

Satan's fourth plan, what I call "spiritual amnesia," is a cunning tactic aimed at causing individuals to forget who they truly are in Christ Jesus. By inducing this forgetfulness, Satan undermines their confidence in God-given rights, spiritual gifts, and authority in Jesus.

Consequently, these individuals begin to accept a lesser role, surrendering their rightful position of royalty to accept the status of a mere servant. They unwittingly choose to be the tail instead of the head, submitting to circumstances instead of rising above them. They become reliant on others, constantly borrowing from them, instead of leading and influencing others.

This spiritual amnesia is a dangerous state, as it prevents believers from fully embracing their true identity and potential in Christ. It blinds them to their inherent power and authority, making them susceptible to Satan's deception and manipulation. Thus, it is crucial for individuals to guard against this plan by continually renewing their minds with God's truth, staying rooted in the Word, and recognizing their divine heritage. Only by remembering and embracing their identity in Christ can believers reclaim their position of spiritual royalty and live a victorious life.

Satan's Fifth Plan: *You're All Alone*

Satan, being the master deceiver, has devised his fifth plan to manipulate the vulnerable mindsets of individuals. His underlying strategy is to make one believe that they are all alone, isolated in their battles. He cunningly erodes the sense of support, making it seem as if those who once stood beside them have abandoned them. But let us take solace in the wisdom gleaned from the scriptures.

In **1st Kings 19:18**, when the servant of God felt he was left alone, God intervened, reassuring him that solitude was merely an illusion. God revealed that there were still seven thousand faithful souls in Israel, refusing to bow down to Baal. This serves as a powerful reminder that we are never truly alone. Even in our darkest moments, God always has someone praying fervently and standing steadfastly by our side.
It is vital to understand that Satan's attempts to convince us of our isolation are mere fabrications designed to exhaust our resilience.

We must always remember that God, in His infinite wisdom, places individuals in our lives to offer support, encouragement, and unwavering companionship. So, whenever you find yourself grappling with the notion of solitude, take comfort in the knowledge that God orchestrates divine connections to uplift and strengthen us, even amidst the fiercest battles.

Satan's Sixth Plan: *You Have No Way Out Of Your Hardship*

Satan's sixth plan is cunning and deceptive. His strategy is to make individuals believe that they have no way of escaping their hardships. This plan is reminiscent of the situation Moses and the Israelites faced when they found themselves trapped between Pharaoh's mighty army and the Red Sea. At first glance, it seemed like an impossible situation, but little did they know that it was all part of God's grand design.

In His miraculous power, God orchestrated an incredible victory. As the Israelites moved forward, God intervened, causing Pharaoh's entire army to be swallowed by the sea. What appeared to be their demise turned into the enemy's downfall.

It serves as a reminder that with every trap that the enemy sets for you, God has the ability to use it for their own destruction. Instead of succumbing to despair, trust in God's plan and His power to turn the tables. Even when it seems like there is no way out, remember that God is always at work, weaving miracles amidst the chaos.

"There has no temptation taken you but such as is common to man: but Yahweh is faithful, who will not suffer you to be tempted above that you are able; but will with the temptation, also make a way to escape, that you may be able to bear it," **1ˢᵗ Corinthians 10:13**.

In other words, God refuses to allow one of His faithful servants, to be tempted above what they're able to handle. If He has delivered millions of people before you, who have been through what you're facing, and even harder things, He is faithful to rescue you as well.

Satan's Seventh Plan: *If Yahweh Had Being Here, This Wouldn't Have Happened*

In the timeless battle between good and evil, Satan's seventh plan is to exploit our moments of pain and suffering, twisting our perception and planting doubt in our hearts. As Martha, the grieving sister of Lazarus, approached Jesus, tears streaming down her face, she couldn't help but utter those words that echoed with the anguish of her soul: "Lord, if you had been here, our brother Lazarus would not have died."

In that moment, Satan reveled, for he desired nothing more than to deceive Martha, to make her believe that her suffering was evidence of God's absence in her life. He wanted her to blame God, to turn away from Him, and seek solace in his deceptive embrace. But unbeknownst to Satan, Jesus saw through his cunning plan.

Instead of succumbing to Martha's despair, Jesus used the situation to reveal the immense power and authority of God. With a voice that echoed through time, Jesus commanded Lazarus to rise from the grave, defying the clutches of death itself. In that miraculous moment, Jesus shattered Satan's illusion and unveiled God's unwavering presence and control over life and death.

The adversary may scheme to make us doubt, to sow seeds of bitterness, and question God's existence in our suffering. Yet, it is Jesus' profound duty to defy Satan's plan, to remind us of the boundless power and love that God holds. Let us remember, even in our darkest moments, it is not God's absence that we should focus on, but rather His incredible ability to bring forth hope, healing, and resurrection.

Satan's Eighth Plan: *Trust The Intel Of Astronomers, Technologies, And The Worldly System Over Yahweh The Bible*

Satan's eighth plan is to encourage the people, particularly Christians, to prioritize accepting the knowledge and findings of astronomers, technologies, and the worldly system over the teachings of the Bible. By promoting this idea, the devil aims to undermine the credibility of the Bible's account of creation, making it seem inaccurate, unreliable, and unrealistic.

This deceptive strategy seeks to discredit God's word, instilling doubt in people's minds not only about the accuracy of the creation story but also about other parts of the Bible. The ultimate goal is to erode people's faith in the entire Bible, convincing them that multiple aspects of scripture are flawed and inaccurate. It's crucial for Christians to recognize this ploy and remain rooted in their belief that the Bible is the infallible word of God, unaffected by the theories and discoveries of man-made systems.

Satan's Nineth Plan: *Destroy The Minds Of Our Children*

Satan's ninth plan is cunningly devised to destroy our children through faulty teaching and lifestyle choices. The Bible explicitly instructs us to raise our children in the right path, promising that they will not deviate from it when they grow older. However, Satan is cunningly manipulating parents into raising their children as fools, with no discipline or accountability.

Mothers, in an attempt to shower their sons with love, are doing them a disservice by providing everything without requiring them to earn it. They cook, clean, iron clothes, and cater to their every whim, fostering a sense of entitlement and laziness. Their sons, expect so much, but when asked to do their chores, complain and are slow at doing them, in addition, they half do them, while expecting a great reward afterwards.

They aren't being taught how to properly contribute to their own family, as a result, these young men grow up seeking partners who will replicate the doting actions of their mothers. When their expectations are not met, they abandon their families, leaving another man to raise up their own children.

Fathers, on the other hand, are abandoning their daughters, leaving them without any positive male role models in their lives. Without proper guidance, these girls lack knowledge of how they should be treated by a man, leading to self-destructive choices. These girls are subject to grow up with unrealistic expectations of what is a real relationship and what defines them as a good woman, besides their proclamation of saying they are.

Mothers are neglecting to teach their daughters the biblical principles of building a strong home, resulting in the dismantling of their own families.

Moreover, in this modern era, many women believe they are valuable based solely on their appearance, failing to recognize the importance of contributing to a relationship beyond physical attributes.

Young boys are subjected to a skewed mindset, where they are taught that the more women they can sleep with, the greater their worth. Little do they know; such behavior is condemned in the Bible and will lead them to the fires of hell.

To protect our children from Satan's destructive plan, it is crucial for parents to prioritize biblical teachings, instill values of discipline and accountability, and guide their children towards building strong, God-centered homes.

Satan's Tenth Plan: *Keep Them On The Defensive, Never On The Offensive*

Satan's tenth plan revolves around keeping people perpetually on the defensive side, rather than adopting an offensive stance. To illustrate this, imagine a basketball game where one team solely focuses on defense, while the opposing team solely focuses on offense.

It becomes predictable who will emerge as the victor. Regardless of how skillfully the defensive team can prevent the opposing team's scoring, eventually, a point will be made against them. The offensive team needs just one successful score to secure victory. In the spiritual realm, Satan's role is to ensure we remain on the defensive, while he and his demons play on the offensive.

As Christians, we often react to the devil when he attacks us directly. However, Satan's strategy involves attacking us in subtle ways that discourage us from fighting back. For instance, if someone says something offensive to us, instead of rebuking the evil spirit behind the attack, we either retaliate with equally harmful words or simply brush it off.
We often fail to recognize the sinister and demonic humor disguised as innocent entertainment on television, laughing along instead of rebuking it. Similarly, when someone blasphemes God's name in a song or on television, we often try to ignore it, but we would readily engage in a fight

if someone insulted our loved ones with similar words.

Satan's plan is to keep us in a defensive state, allowing his influence to persist and grow. It is essential for us to recognize his tactics and begin actively fighting back against the spiritual warfare he wages.

Satan's Eleventh Plan: *Let Me Change Who You Are, But I Will Remain The Same*

Satan's eleventh plan is deviously clever, for it capitalizes on a person's weakness to see flaws in others while neglecting their own self-improvement. This cunning strategy thrives on the satisfaction Satan obtains when someone tirelessly attempts to change those around them, all while remaining stagnant themselves. It's a devious dance, where the individual skillfully avoids taking responsibility for their own faults, regardless of how clearly, they're in the wrong.

These individuals possess a remarkable capability to deflect blame, constantly redirecting it onto others, rather than facing their own shortcomings. Their insidious demands for undivided attention exemplify the relentless nature of Satan's plan.

They insist on being heard, their voice dominating every conversation, yet when it comes to listening to others, they never fail to interrupt and drown out opposing viewpoints.

The perpetual victimhood they embrace allows them to navigate life without ever undergoing self-reflection or personal growth.

In Satan's ever-evolving repertoire of strategies, the eleventh plan stands as a testament to his mastery of manipulation. It exploits a fundamental flaw in human nature, fueling an unending cycle of stagnancy and discontent.

Satan's Twelfth Plan: *Waterdown The Gospel*

Satan's twelfth plan revolves around his cunning strategy to Waterdown the gospel. Aware that he cannot entirely halt the preaching and teaching of the gospel, he aims to exert influence upon ministers to dilute its core essence. To achieve this, he manipulates them into omitting crucial aspects such as the true meaning of repentance, the significance of living a holy life, the pursuit of a sin-free lifestyle, the art of effectively combating evil forces, and the unquestionable reality of a fiery hell.

In today's context, it is alarming to witness people comfortably mingling with pastors without feeling any guilt for their sinful ways, as they obtain tacit approval from the ministers themselves. The focus of preachers has shifted, as they prioritize delivering a message that brings joy to their congregation rather than impelling them towards freedom.

Rather than disclosing the bitter truth that prompts individuals to confront their transgressions and seek repentance, preachers opt for a feel-good sermon—one that avoids causing discomfort or the need for soul-searching. Their concern lies more in assessing their own performance rather than genuinely caring whether their listeners will strive for holiness and wholeheartedly surrender themselves to God.

Satan's Thirteenth Plan: *You Can Do It Tomorrow*

One of Satan's most deceptive schemes is his preying on people's tendency to procrastinate with the notion that they can simply do it tomorrow. However, the stark truth is that tomorrow is never promised to anyone. Life is fragile, and one can be here today and gone the next minute. Our time is both limited and precious, a valuable resource that should not be taken for granted.

Sadly, procrastination has become all too prevalent in this day and age. Many individuals embrace the belief that if something isn't easy, they won't even bother trying. Satan preys on this weakness, whispering the seductive lie that there's always another day to get things done. This deceptive mindset can trap us in a never-ending loop of missed opportunities and unfulfilled dreams.

We must realize that time is not infinite, and each moment lost can never be regained. So, let us resist the temptation of Satan's thirteenth plan and seize the present, making the most of the time we have been granted. Let us break free from the chains of procrastination and live a life filled with purpose and accomplishment. Remember, tomorrow may never come, so act now and make your days count.

Satan's Fourteenth Plan: *No Forgiveness*

Satan's fourteenth plan is a sinister continuation of his relentless pursuit to keep individuals trapped within the confines of their own mistakes. It is his primary duty to ensure that each person remains imprisoned within their self-imposed condemnation. Every single day, his army of demons work tirelessly to tempt individuals into committing significant errors. Once a mistake is made, Satan orchestrates the placement of people around them who will continuously remind them of their past transgressions, treating them as nothing more than the embodiment of their missteps.

Even if those surrounding the person refuse to execute them, a systematic record is meticulously maintained. This record remains accessible to anyone online, enabling them to delve into the depths of a person's negative history. It matters not whether the individual has already paid their societal debts or if the crime occurred years ago; Satan's insidious agenda remains unwavering. He assumes the role of the accuser, exploiting every opportunity to drag individuals into a perpetual cycle of shame and guilt.
Beware of this cunning scheme, for its purpose is to ensure that no soul can escape the grip of condemnation and find redemption.

Even among those who claim to be Christians, forgiveness is elusive. They are quick to demand God's forgiveness for their own sins, yet unwilling to extend the same grace to others who have erred.

It is disheartening to witness how some treat their fellow human beings with less compassion than they would an animal, simply because of past mistakes. However, when these very individuals are caught in their own wrongdoing, their tune suddenly changes. Much like the biblical account of David and the prophet Nathan, who exposed David's own guilt in having a man killed to be with his wife, there is a stark contrast in their response.

When David thought the judgment was for someone else, he thirsted for justice. But when the truth was revealed, and the finger pointed at himself, mercy and forgiveness were his desperate plea. This same pattern persists today, where people clamor for judgment when they believe it applies to another, yet seek great mercy and understanding when they realize they are at fault.

Satan uses this stark hypocrisy to keep individuals trapped in condemnation. By perpetuating a cycle of judgment without forgiveness, he fuels division and bitterness, preventing true healing and reconciliation. It is imperative that we break free from this deceitful plan and embrace a spirit of mercy, forgiveness, and understanding, whether it pertains to ourselves or others. Only then can we escape from the clutches of condemnation and experience the freedom and redemption that God offers.

Satan's Fifteenth Plan: *Keep The People In Ignorance*

Satan's fifteenth plan revolves around perpetuating ignorance among the masses, as it is the very foundation that empowers all demons. These malevolent entities thrive on people's lack of awareness, ensuring that they either deny their existence altogether or underestimate their importance. By dismissing demons as mere figments of imagination, individuals are less inclined to confront them head-on. Instead, they unwittingly channel their energy into battling other humans, diverting attention away from the true source of evil.

Through strategic manipulation, Satan seeks to veil the truth and keep humanity oblivious to the sinister forces at play. When people remain oblivious, they inadvertently become conduits for the malevolence demons inhabit, enabling them to carry out their wicked intentions undeterred. By fostering an environment of ignorance, Satan aims to maintain his stronghold, maneuvering from the shadows and exercising his influence with minimal resistance.

To combat this nefarious plan, it becomes imperative for individuals to acknowledge the existence and significance of these demonic entities. Only through awareness and understanding can they actively resist their control and protect themselves from falling prey to their wicked machinations. By breaking free from the chains of ignorance, the world can gradually weaken Satan's grasp, paving the way for enlightenment and liberation from his insidious influence.

Satan's Sixth Plan: *Hearer, But Never A Doer*

Satan's sixteenth plan is cunningly devised to ensnare individuals who, albeit attending church and regularly reading their Bible, are deceived into merely hearing the word of God but never becoming doers of it. His objective lies in thwarting their progress from mere knowledge to actual application, rendering their efforts futile and void of spiritual growth. The adversary fully comprehends that attending church and flipping through scripture is inconsequential if one fails to translate their understanding into tangible actions.

By withholding scriptural teachings from transcending theoretical realms, Satan effectively burdens these individuals with a mere semblance of godliness or religiosity. Their faith becomes stagnant, devoid of the transformative power intended by the word of God. The cunning nature of Satan's plan lies in the subtlety with which it undermines the foundation of an individual's spiritual journey, replacing vibrant obedience with stagnant observance.

To truly combat this scheme, it is crucial to wholeheartedly embrace the word of God, allowing it to guide actions, decisions, and relationships. Combining the hearing and doing of the word solidifies one's faith, propelling them towards true spiritual growth and an unwavering commitment to a life anchored in God's truth.

Satan's Seventeenth Plan: *Prepare Their Hearts For His Son's Appearance*

Satan's seventeenth plan, as foretold in **Revelation 13:1**, involves a strategic scheme aimed at preparing the hearts of the people for the arrival of Satan's son, the antichrist. The biblical passage reveals that the beast rose from the sea of people, symbolizing the emergence of the antichrist under Satan's guidance. With his vast power and authority bestowed by the dragon himself, the antichrist is destined to exert control over a significant portion of the world.

Unlike Yahweh, who respects humanity's free will by granting them the choice to worship him or not, the antichrist will adopt a totalitarian approach. He will demand unwavering devotion, leaving no room for alternatives, under the dreadful consequence of death for those who resist his reign.

Satan's grand design encompasses a meticulous cultivation of people's hearts, instilling fear, disillusionment, and an insidious allure of power and false promises. By appealing to their deepest vulnerabilities and exploiting their weaknesses, Satan aims to manipulate and deceive the masses, paving the way for the establishment of his son's oppressive regime.

Vigilance, discernment, and a steadfast commitment to truth and righteousness will prove vital in resisting Satan's unholy agenda, as the battle between darkness and light intensifies in the approaching era of the antichrist.

Satan's Eighteenth Plan: *Practice Any Other Religion Expect For Christianity*

Satan's eighteenth plan is devious yet cunningly simple: encouraging people to practice yoga or any other religion, except for Christianity. His motive remains consistent since his fall from heaven, for Satan desires worship. No other religion can boast about casting out demons, opening blinded eyes, raising the dead, healing the sick, walking on water, and setting captives free like Christianity, Satan exploits these alternative religions to achieve his sinister goals, primarily secret worship.

Through yoga and other spiritual practices, Satan veils his true intentions under the guise of seeking enlightenment and inner peace. Unbeknownst to its followers, these practices subtly divert their devotion away from the true Creator and towards sinister forces. By luring individuals towards any belief system that rejects Christ's teachings, Satan skillfully undermines the saving power of Christianity and perpetuates his deceptive influence.

It is imperative for believers to discern Satan's cunning plan and remain vigilant against spiritual deception.

Satan's Nineteenth Plan: *Stop The Light From Shining And The Fire From Burning*

Yeshua said, *"You are the light of the world. A city that is set on a hill cannot be hid. Neither do men light a candle, and put it under a bushel, but on a candlestick; and it gives light unto all that are in the house. Let your light so shine before men, that they may see your good works, and glorify your Father which is in heaven,"* **Matthew 5:14-16**.

The devil wants to put out your light by showing you things that appears to be working against you, instead of for you. *"The lamp of the body is the eye. If therefore your eye is good, your whole body will be full of light. But if your eye is bad, your whole body will be full of darkness. If therefore the light that is in you is darkness, how great is that darkness!"* **Matthew 6:22-23**.

Therefore, if you could see in the spirit, you would see yourself shining with the light of God upon you, and this is how the devil can identify you. Whenever the demons see the light, they are assigned to put it out.

Let's go deeper, the gospel of **Matthew 3:11-12** says, "*I indeed baptize you with water unto repentance, but He who is coming after me is mightier than I. He will baptize you with the Holy Spirit and fire.*"
Ergo, not only do demons see the light of Yeshua upon you, you are burning with the fire from the Holy Ghost upon you.

Yeshua declared that believers are the light of the world, for He has baptized us with the Holy Ghost and Fire. When the enemy gazes at a born-again follower, they see a radiant light and burning fire. The more one surrenders to Yahweh and aligns with the teachings of the Bible, the brighter that light shines and the more intense the fire of God becomes. The adversary, upon noticing this powerful light, deploys his minions to combat it and attempts to extinguish it.

Demons vigilantly observe the individual, scrutinizing for vulnerabilities, and once identified, launch assaults in those areas. In this spiritual battle, standing firm in faith and resisting the attacks is crucial to keep the light and fire burning brightly.

Satan's Twentieth Plan: *To Take Human Out Of Yahweh*

Satan's plan is to take humans from their source so they can die spiritually. Mankind was made in the image of Yahweh. When God wanted fish, he spoke to the sea and created them in the water. If you take a fish out of what it was created in, it will live shortly and then die. When God wanted trees, he spoke to the soil and created them in the soil. If you take a tree from where it was created in, which is the soil, it will soon die. When God wanted humans, he spoke to himself and created them.
If you take man from where he was created, he will live temporarily and then die shortly because he cannot live from out of where he was created, and the devil knows this.
When a person forsakes the word of Yahweh, he will die spiritually first, and if he doesn't return, his body will die, then he will perish in hell of fire.

Satan's Twenty-First Plan: *To View Yahweh And His Saints From Their Perspective*

Demons are overwhelmed with joy whenever they can persuade a person, especially a one-time believer in God, to now see Him and His saints from their wicked perspective - with great hatred. They desire to teach people how to become offended at the Creator, just as they are. In their twisted worldview, they want all of us to see Yahweh and His saints through their malevolent lens, spreading their toxic influence and sowing seeds of doubt and animosity towards the divine. Stay vigilant against their deceptions and remember that true understanding comes from love and light, not from the darkness that demons seek to veil our hearts with.

Satan's Twenty-Second Plan: *Create Forms Of Godliness*

Satan has trained individuals to infiltrate the church under the guise of holiness and righteousness. These impostors have a form of godliness but deny its true power. They are hearers of the gospel, but not doers of it. They masquerade as Christ, performing deceitful miracles to mislead believers. Some have even managed to rise to positions of authority within the church, preaching and teaching the gospel while posing as pastors. However, they are nothing more than wolves in sheep's clothing, seeking to sow confusion and discord among true believers. It is crucial for discerning followers to stay vigilant and rooted in genuine faith to avoid falling prey to these cunning deceivers.

Keep the people in religion, but never allow them assets to salvation. Let them experience a form of religion.

Satan's Twenty-Third Plan: *Divide And Conquer*

One of Satan's greatest weapons used to establish his kingdom is racism. The senseless and countless deaths attributed to racism, as well as the destruction of innocent lives, are undeniable consequences. Wars, genocides, and ethnic cleansing are often fueled by this divisive behavior. Regrettably, racism has infiltrated our churches, where instead of addressing it head-on, many choose to turn a blind eye. This insidious prejudice is also prevalent in the corporate world, leading to qualified individuals being unfairly passed over due to their skin color. Families have even rejected their own kin for choosing to marry someone of a different race. Racism not only shattered lives on an individual level but also poses a grave threat to the unity and prosperity of nations.

Satan's Twenty-Fourth Plan: *Instead Of Worshipping Idols, Idolize People*

In times past, people would worship false deities such as idols, things made from wood, stones, or from jewelry, but nowadays, Satan has convinced them to worship certain people and worldly possessions. If Satan cannot convince the people to worship others, then they are to give most of their limited time to foolish things, playing video games for hours, listening and dancing to music that's highly offensive or depressing, entertainment, and social media.

But this is no different than the demons, who choose Lucifer's gifts over Yahweh's holiness. The allure of materialism and the false promises of temporary pleasure have blinded many to the true essence of spirituality, leading them away from the path of righteousness.

Satan's Twenty-Fifth Plan: *Cause Lack Of Emotional Intelligence*

The lack of emotional intelligence prevailing in our world today is unsettling. Satan's influence is leading millions of individuals to make life-altering decisions solely driven by their fleeting emotions. This emotional instability is causing chaos and confusion, hindering rational thinking and sound judgment.
It is imperative for individuals to cultivate emotional intelligence to navigate the complexities of life and make informed choices that align with their values and goals. By developing self-awareness, self-regulation, empathy, and social skills, we can counter the detrimental impact of emotional impulsivity and create a more harmonious and understanding society.

Satan's Twenty-Sixth Plan: *Corrupt The Minds Of Western Women*

In the book of **Isaiah 4:1**, it is prophesied that in the last days, women will face a great shame as reflected in their unreasonable and delusional behaviors. The scripture describes a scene where seven women will seek one man, not for love or companionship, but merely to escape disgrace by taking on his name. This prophecy resonates with the current state of affairs, especially in Western society, where some women exhibit entitlement and skewed beliefs in relationships.

Many expect their partners to provide for them while refusing to contribute equally. This imbalance reveals a societal shift where traditional gender roles are questioned yet expected to be upheld selectively. The upcoming challenges women face highlight the importance of reevaluating societal norms and fostering mutual respect and understanding in relationships."

In our western society, most younger women would rather be sexually active with a man and bear his children, rather than getting up and fixing him a sandwich.

Satan's Twenty-Seventh Plan: *Destroy Our Young Men*

Satan is actively working to destroy our young men. In a society where most men grow up without a father figure, the absence leaves their mothers to juggle dual roles, often struggling to provide the necessary guidance and discipline. As a result, many mothers inadvertently harm their sons by allowing them to become complacent, failing to teach essential life skills like cooking, cleaning, and respectful behavior towards women.

Consequently, these young men grow up seeking partners reminiscent of their mothers, expecting them to cater to their needs without reciprocation. If they are attractive, they may become womanizers, engaging in relationships without commitment, leading to multiple children with different partners. Toxic friendships further enable their reckless and irresponsible behavior, perpetuating a cycle of abandonment akin to their own fathers' actions, perpetuating a destructive pattern through generations.

Satan's Twenty-Eighth Plan: *Destroy Through Our Worldly System*

The infiltration of Satan through our worldly system is evident in the laws being enacted, defying the principles of the Bible and provoking the wrath of the Lord God. These laws endorse same-sex marriages, allow transgender individuals to compete in women's sports and invade women's spaces, and unjustly favor women in divorce proceedings regardless of fault. This malevolent scheme aims to discourage men from marrying women.
It promotes the blasphemous notion of accepting homosexual unions and even permits some homosexuals to serve as pastors, falsely claiming divine approval for their sinful conduct. Moreover, it deceitfully convinces women that abortion is permissible, despite being a grave sin in the eyes of Yahweh. Beware of the subtle workings of evil, for Satan's influence is pervasive and insidious.

Satan's Twenty-Ninth Plan: *Hinder The Prayers*

Satan wants to hinder a person's prayers because if he can disrupt their communication with Yahweh, he can weaken their connection to the divine. One way he achieves this is by sowing discord between a husband and wife.

By creating division and preventing resolution of their issues, Satan ensures that when they pray, their communication with God is obstructed. This tactic plays on the power of unity and harmony in prayer, showing how Satan exploits relationships to hinder spiritual connection. It serves as a reminder of the importance of maintaining strong bonds and resolving conflicts to protect one's spiritual well-being from such interference.

Satan's Thirty Plan: *It's all about you*

"It's all about you," whispered Satan, urging the person to focus solely on themselves and disregard the feelings and opinions of others. He cunningly persuaded them to surround themselves with like-minded individuals who validate their selfish ways, ensuring they remain unchanged.

Satan's ultimate goal is to foster a sense of self-centeredness, trapping them in a cycle of egotism and preventing personal growth and empathy towards others. Beware of falling into the trap of making everything about yourself, for it is a path that leads away from compassion and understanding."

Satan's Thirty-First Plan: *Returning Back*

Returning back to where God has delivered you from is a dangerous path to tread. In the biblical narrative of Moses leading the Israelites to freedom from Egypt, we see a pattern emerge when hardships arise in the wilderness. Instead of turning to Yahweh, who orchestrated their liberation, the Israelites grumble and direct their anger towards Moses.

This serves as a stark reminder that the enemy's tactic is to lure us back to the chains we have been freed from. Just as the Israelites longed to return to captivity, demons aim to steer us away from our deliverance. It is crucial to remain steadfast in our faith and trust in God's guidance, resisting the temptation to revisit past struggles that God has already brought us out of.

The Five Star Demonic

1. Do to others, what they have done to you. Forgive only those who deserves it.

Rely upon your feelings, and act upon them. Let your heart be your guide.

Suppress no desire. If it pleases your fleshly needs, yield to it. Just don't get caught.

Judge others in accordance to what you have heard, read about, how they look, talk, the color of their skin and appearance.

Help only those who serve your interest, but to those who aren't able to aid you or they're poor and needy, avoid.
But if you need the poor peoples in order to get ahead, to gain power and authority, sell them a false dream; make them believe that you care, but once you win, that same day, forget every promise you have made to them.

CASE TWELVE *Christian's Spiritual Weapons & Armors*

<u>Ephesians 6:14-17</u>, unveils our spiritual armor. Our spiritual weapons and armors weren't given to us just to make us look good, but rather for us to employ them in combat against the forces of evil. These divine provisions are our arsenal for spiritual warfare, consisting of the following:

- First, we have the belt of truth, securing our core and enabling us to discern falsehood from truth amidst the deceptive schemes of the enemy.

- Next is the breastplate of righteousness, protecting our hearts and ensuring we live with integrity and godliness, guarding us against the attacks on our character and moral standing.

- Our feet are equipped with the preparation of the gospel of peace, enabling us to be ready to share and promote the message of salvation, serving as ambassadors for Christ wherever we go.

- No battle is complete without the shield of faith, designed to deflect the wicked one's fiery darts of doubt, fear, and temptation, providing steadfast confidence in God's promises.

- Our spiritual armor includes the helmet of salvation, guarding our minds against the enemy's lies and securing our eternal destiny in Christ.

- Lastly, we wield the sword of the spirit, which is the word of God, a powerful offensive weapon to defeat the enemy's strongholds, demolishing every false argument and exposing the lies.

Let us not merely adorn ourselves with these spiritual weapons and armors but actively engage in the battle, fighting for truth, righteousness, peace, and the eternal souls of mankind.

"For though we walk in the flesh, we do not war after the flesh [with physical weapons]. *For the weapons of our warfare are not carnal* [fleshly], *but mighty through Yahweh to the **pulling down of strongholds**; **casting down imaginations**, and **every high thing that exalts itself against the knowledge of Yahweh**, and **bringing into captivity every thought** to the **obedience of Christ**," 2nd Corinthians 10:3-5*.

You might have noticed that our weapons possess the capabilities to do five things, with correlates to the five things that Lucifer said he would do. So, let's see how this looks:

Lucifer's Word	_Our Weapons_
1. I will ascend into heaven	1. Pulling down of strongholds
2. I will exalt my throne above the stars of God	2. Casting down imaginations
3. I will also sit on the mount of the congregation, on the far Sides of the north	3. Every high thing that exalts itself against the knowledge of Yahweh
4. I will ascend above the heights of The clouds	4. Bringing into captivity every thought
5. I will be like the Most-High	5. To the obedience of Christ

Pulling Down Stronghold, Greek word [3794. ochuróma] which means: fortress. Usage: a fortress strong defense, stronghold. Ergo, the first weapon that a Christian has, is the ability to pull down {demolish, destroy, overcome, and reduce} the strongholds {fortress or strong defense} in their life.

In **_Ephesians 6:14-17_**, this stronghold is referred to arguments; the negative inner voices that tries to convince the person to do either think and or, behave wrongly, or someone else's negative influences. Whatsoever argument that comes to an individual's mind, the hamlet of salvation will be able to withstand the blow.

Casing Down Imaginations, Greek word [5325. phantasia] which means: to show, display. Our spiritual weapons, bestowed upon us by the gracious Holy Spirit, possess the incredible power to cast down the nefarious imaginations that may infiltrate our minds.

Regardless of the negative thoughts or malicious suggestions that the devil cunningly attempts to implant, we wield a formidable weapon, capable of neutralizing such insidious attacks. It serves as a divine shield, safeguarding our thoughts and repelling any malevolent influences. In the face of doubt, fear, or any other negative force that seeks to consume our minds, we stand firm, armed with the transcendent strength of our spiritual weapons.

With unwavering faith and the empowering guidance of the Holy Spirit, we confidently reject and dispel any debilitating thoughts, replacing them with thoughts of love, hope, and righteousness. United with our spiritual weaponry, we rise above the machinations of the enemy and conquer the battlefield of the mind.

Every high thing that exalts it knowledge against Yahweh: In our journey of faith, we have been bestowed with a remarkable spiritual weapon that functions like a radar, constantly seeking out anything that dares to exalt itself against the knowledge of Yahweh. This extraordinary tool acts as a divine alarm, sensitizing our souls to anything that attempts to claim a higher position than God in our lives. With each detection, it empowers us to become aware, alert, and vigilant.

Armed with this spiritual radar, we are now capable of identifying every high thing that arrogantly elevates itself against the wisdom and sovereignty of our Lord. As we tap into this profound awareness, we are enabled to confront and dismantle such opposing forces. Let us be steadfast in our commitment to humbly submit to Yahweh's supremacy, and with unwavering determination, let us bring down every stronghold that dares to rise against Him.

May this spiritual radar serve as a constant reminder of our allegiance and devotion to Yahweh, allowing us to discern and combat anything that challenges His divine authority in our lives.

Bringing into captivity every thought *to the* **_obedience of Christ_**: In the battle between good and evil, the devil cunningly seeks to hinder our spiritual growth by discouraging the study and application of God's Word. The devil knows that when we diligently explore and internalize the teachings of the Bible, our thoughts become obedient to Christ.

As believers, we are called to bring every thought into captivity, aligning them with the divine principles revealed to us. By resisting the devil's schemes, we can maintain a steadfast focus on Christ's teachings, ensuring that our minds continually submit to His authority.

The word of God has transformative power, guiding our thoughts away from worldly concerns and redirecting them towards godliness. Through the diligent study of Scripture, we gain insight into God's desires for our lives, allowing us to resist the devil's attempts to deceive and distract us. By faithfully applying the wisdom and guidance found in the Bible, we bring our thoughts into alignment with Christ, fostering a mindful life that honors God and reflects His love to the world.

Putting On The Whole Armor of Yahweh

Having Grided Your Waist With Truth: In the powerful words of Jesus, he proclaimed, "I am the way, the truth, and the life." It is through this unwavering truth that we find guidance and purpose in our lives. When we consciously choose to walk in truth, we invite the spirit of Jesus to take the lead, to guide our steps, and to shape our decisions.

Jesus Himself emphasized the importance of knowing the truth, for it possesses the remarkable ability to set us free. It is in the embrace of truth that we release ourselves from the chains of deception and illusion, finding liberation and clarity of mind. By aligning ourselves with the truth of Jesus, we discover a strength within us that enables us to navigate life's challenges and triumph over adversity.

We are encouraged to grid our waist with truth, to gird ourselves with the teachings and principles revealed by Jesus. By doing so, we become anchored in an unshakable foundation that brings forth transformation and empowers us to live authentically. May we continually seek the truth, allowing it to shape our thoughts, actions, and beliefs, so that we may experience the true freedom and abundant life offered through Jesus's loving guidance.

Breastplate of Righteousness: The Breastplate of Righteousness serves as a powerful shield, designed to protect our heart, mind, and spirit. As followers of Yahweh, we are called to walk in His righteousness, aligning our thoughts, actions, and beliefs with His divine will. It is not enough to simply do what feels right to us; our obedience lies in adhering to His holy word.

Wearing the Breastplate of Righteousness signifies our commitment to living a life in harmony with Yahweh's truth. It reminds us that our hearts are guarded against the temptations of the world, shielding us from the deceptive whispers that seek to lead us astray. When we choose righteousness, we choose to stand firm on the solid foundation of His commands.

In this journey, we find solace in knowing that Yahweh's righteousness envelops us, offering protection and guidance. May the Breastplate of Righteousness serve as a constant reminder of our duty to walk in His ways, ensuring that our actions reflect obedience and our hearts remain steadfast in His love.

Having shod your feet with the Preparation of the Gospel of Peace: Having shod your feet with the Preparation of the Gospel of Peace is a powerful concept mentioned in the Bible. This phrase encompasses a deeper meaning that pertains to three distinctive types of peace.

The first is peace with God, which arises when we fully surrender ourselves to Him. It involves trusting in His guidance, seeking His will, and finding solace in His presence. This profound surrender brings a sense of tranquility, knowing that God is in control and is faithfully fighting for us.

The second type is the peace of God, which surpasses all understanding. In the midst of chaos and turmoil, this peace prevails as an inner serenity. It acts as a shield, allowing us to remain calm and secure, despite external circumstances. This peace comes from the assurance that God is our protector, defender, and provider.

Lastly, we have peace with humans. Remarkably, when we have this deep connection with God, He can even bring about reconciliation and harmony with our enemies. He has the power to soften hearts and bridge gaps, transforming hostility into friendship, and paving the way for understanding and peace.

In summary, by being grounded in the Preparation of the Gospel of Peace, we are equipped to navigate life's challenges. We experience peace with God, peace of God, and peace with humans, embracing a life of faith, trust, and reconciliation.

Shield of Faith: The shield of faith, as the Bible teaches us, possesses the remarkable power to defend us against all of Satan's fiery darts. It stands as our impenetrable barrier, safeguarding us from every dirty trick the enemy hurls our way. Without this shield, every cunning scheme plotted against us by the adversary would undoubtedly find victory. But faith serves a purpose beyond demonic encounters; it also serves as our armor when doubt creeps into our hearts.

Indeed, Scripture affirms that without faith, it is impossible to please God. Those who seek a relationship with Him must believe not only in His existence but also that He rewards those who diligently seek Him. With faith as our ally, we possess the ability to speak to the mountains in our lives, and witness their miraculous movement. Our dreams and aspirations find fulfillment when we accompany them with bold and resolute actions that stem from our unwavering faith.

Let us, therefore, hold up the shield of faith in all aspects of our lives, trusting in its power to defend us in spiritual battles and provide a solid foundation for our dreams.

The Helmet of Salvation: Every day, the mind becomes a battlefield, where the clash between good and evil takes place. Satan and his cunning demons relentlessly strive to infiltrate our thoughts, aiming to gain control. They understand that by controlling the mind, they can dictate our decisions, choices, and ultimately shape the outcomes we experience. Whether it is within the confines of a family, a nation, or an entire kingdom, the battleground remains the same.

Before a punch is thrown or a kick is executed, the real fight begins within our minds. It is here that victories or defeats are determined, long before battle plans are drawn or weapons are fired. The power struggle hinges upon the thoughts we entertain and the beliefs we hold. If we allow our minds to be dominated by negative forces, the consequences can ripple through every aspect of our lives.

Recognizing this, we must remain vigilant and guard our minds against the influences of darkness. By fortifying our thoughts by receiving the mind of Christ, wearing the helmet of salvation, faith, and righteousness, we can protect ourselves and influence the world around us. That way, we contribute to building a stronger, brighter tomorrow, free from the grip of demonic influences.

Whenever a believer wears the helmet of salvation, he or she is able to destroy whatever argument that comes to their mind, whether it be a demon speaking to their mind, or an external enemy.

The Sword of the Spirit: The Sword of the Spirit, as stated in the Scriptures, is not merely the ability to recite biblical verses with fluency, but it encompasses a way of life. It goes beyond the mere intellectual knowledge of the Word, for it is written that we should not live by bread alone, but by every word that emanates from the mouth of Yahweh.

This mighty sword possesses the power to slice through the forces of evil and inflict great harm upon the devils that plague our existence. Its blade is sharp and unyielding, fueled by the teachings and commands of our Creator. It is a divine weapon bestowed upon us, enabling us to confront the darkness that seeks to envelop us.

To wield this sacred weapon effectively, we must embrace and integrate the essence of the Scriptures into our daily lives. We must embody its teachings, allowing it to guide our actions, decisions, and interactions. With the Sword of the Spirit in our hands, we become warriors in the battle against the malevolent forces of the spiritual realm, bringing light, truth, and victory wherever we go.

Praying always with all prayer and supplication in the spirit: In the book of Ephesians, the apostle Paul encourages us to engage in constant prayer and supplication, guided by the Holy Spirit. The Bible teaches us that prayer should permeate every aspect of our lives. It is an essential channel of communication between us and God. However, we are also reminded to align our prayers with God's will for us. It is crucial to approach prayer with humility and a desire to seek his purpose rather than our own desires.

When we pray in accordance with his will, we can have confidence that he hears us. Our prayers become powerful, as they align with his divine plan for our lives. As believers, we are called to develop a habit of continual and spirit-led prayer, acknowledging God's sovereignty while seeking his guidance and intervention in every situation. May we always remember the importance of praying always, with all prayer and supplication, in the spirit. **Ephesians 6:13-18**.

Now that you have completely this book on demons, esteemed gentlemen and ladies of the general assembly, what say you? Have I succeeded in persuading you to declare war upon demons immediately, acknowledging their wickedness beyond one's imagination? Or have I failed to convince you?
Let us not dwell solely on the evil that demons embody, but rather let us consider taking action, just as our Lord and Savior Jesus did when faced with such darkness. Demons, vile and cunning as they are, require a decisive response from us.

The choice, dear assembly members, lies in your capable hands. Shall we continue mere discussions about the severity of their wickedness? Or shall we rise together, united in purpose, and confront this menace head-on? The time has come to make a stand against these unholy forces. Will you join me in this righteous battle?"

Thank you for purchasing the book titled "Satan's Sinister Scheme For Humanity's Demise." I hope that this book ignites a fire within you to stand against the forces of evil, become a beacon of light in the darkness, and encourage others to join the battle against demons. May its contents inspire you to recognize and combat the devil's deceitful schemes, empowering you to make a difference in the spiritual warfare. Let us unite in our fight against darkness and work towards a brighter, more enlightened future. Thank you for your support and may this book be a powerful tool in your journey towards spiritual awakening and empowerment.
If you wish to contact me, you can at:
Truthbookspresents@gmail.com

www.ingramcontent.com/pod-product-compliance
Lightning Source LLC
Chambersburg PA
CBHW060155050426
42446CB00013B/2837